Prayers from Around the World and Across the Ages

Compiled by
Victor M. Parachin

Foreword by
Gregory F. Augustine Pierce

ACTA
ASSISTING CHRISTIANS TO ACT
PUBLICATIONS

Prayers from Around the World and Across the Ages
Compiled by Victor M. Parachin, M. Div

Foreword by Gregory F. Augustine Pierce

Edited by Andrew Yankech
Cover design by Tom A. Wright
Typesetting by Desktop Edit Shop, Inc.
Cover photo used under rights granted to Seescapes Publishing

See "Works Consulted" for sources of prayers and permissions received. Any errors or omissions will be corrected in future editions.

Published by: ACTA Publications
                 Assisting Christians To Act
                 4848 N. Clark Street
                 Chicago, IL 60640
                 773-271-1030
                 actapublications@aol.com
                 www.actapublications.com

Library of Congress Number: 2004110460
ISBN: 0-87946-272-8
Printed in the United States of America
Year: 09 08 07 06 05 04
Printing: 10 9 8 7 6 5 4 3 2 1

Contents

Foreword

Communicating with the holy, the sacred, the divine, the transcendent, the ultimately meaningful power of the universe is daunting at best, presumptuous at worst. Who are we as humans to know the mind of God, much less how God wants to be addressed? Prayer is difficult enough when we use our own words.

When we add to that problem by trying to pray the prayers of other people—especially people of different backgrounds, times and even religions—we are really asking for trouble. After all, what do we have in common spiritually with John Bunyan, Jane Austin, W. E. B. DuBois, Etty Hillesum and Thich Nhat Hanh, not to mention Mechthild of Magdenburg, Rabindranath Tagore, Toyohiko Kagawa and the Metropolitan Philaret of Moscow? How are the prayers of Woodrow Wilson, Johannes Scotus of Erigena, Elizabeth of Hungary, Ludwig van Beethoven and Florence Nightingale going to help us in this day and this age?

The answer may lie in these wonderful *Prayers from Around the World and Across the Ages,* compiled by Victor Parachin. The author is an inveterate collector of prayers, but he is equally as interested in the identity and motivation of the pray-ers. He has carefully and assiduously searched for people who have lived life to the fullest and in the process raised their voices in prayer for a plethora of causes and occasions. He not only presents their prayers, but also insightful mini-biographies of who they were and where they were coming from as they "lifted their minds and hearts to God."

Why might it be valuable to our own prayer life to read and pray these prayers? They deal with all aspects of the human condition, and they do so from the finely tuned sensibilities of individuals who have a highly developed faith and spirituality. These prayers can help us learn how to pray in all situations—perhaps not "better" or more "effectively," but with more heart, more passion and certainly more love. God's got to like that.

So enjoy this unique and compelling collection of the prayers of others...and perhaps make some of them your own.

Gregory F. Augustine Pierce
Co-Publisher, ACTA Publications

Introduction

This book of prayers differs from most other prayer books in two distinct ways: First, the prayers are preceded by a brief biography of the person who wrote the prayer. Second, the prayers in this book come from people of faith in various religious traditions. While most of the prayers cited are Christian, also included are prayers from other households of faith. It should be noted that Eastern religions (Buddhist, Hindu, Tao, Confuciansism) stress meditation rather than prayer as we know it in the West. Thus there is not the same body of prayers available from which to select. Nevertheless, several prayers, blessings, meditative poems and litanies from Eastern faiths are included in order to acquaint Christians with the spirituality of people from the East. Their expressions point toward an Ultimate Transcendent Reality with whom they hope to lovingly connect.

These prayers come from a wide range and diversity of individuals: some were clearly devout, while others were driven to prayer by necessity; some were ordained and in full-time religious work, while others were lay people with a remarkable piety; some were theologically trained and sophisticated, while others had limited theological knowledge but considerable spiritual wisdom and awareness; some are well known, while others are nearly invisible in the public arena. Common to all, however, is the profound awareness of God and the deep desire to be in union with the Divine.

Victor M. Parachin

argery Kempe (1373-1439) suffered mental illness after the birth of her first child. A vision of Christ, she said, brought healing to her mind and spirit. She subsequently had another thirteen children. Her father was John Burnham, mayor of Lynn, England. She married John Kempe in 1393. With his consent she separated from him and went on a pilgrimage, visting English shrines, mystics and the Holy Land. She returned to Lynn in 1425 in order to care for her ill husband. After his death she continued on pilgrimages. A distinct aspect of her mysticism was crying in public, an activity for which she was often ridiculed and dismissed. Kempe explained that her tears were ones of compassion for the suffering of others and her identification with the suffering of Christ. An effective speaker, she defended herself with wit and courage against various clerical attacks made upon her. At the end of her life, she dictated her life story to secretaries. Titled *The Book of Margery Kempe,* it is considered the first autobiography in English. The book was lost for almost five hundred years until an early copy was discovered in 1934. The book contains many fascinating encounters between Kempe and God, including this divine exhortation: "Our merciful Lord, speaking to her inwardly, reproached her for her fear, saying: 'Why are you so afraid? I am as mighty here on the sea as on the land. Why do you mistrust me? All that I have promised you I will surely fulfill, and I will never deceive you.'"

For Patience, Peace and Courage in Suffering:

Dear Lord, *you suffered so much pain*
in order to save me and all mankind from sin.
Yet I find it hard to bear even this little pain in my body.
Lord, because of your great pain, have mercy on my little pain.
And if you wish me simply to bear the pain,
send me the patience and courage which I lack.
It may seem strange to say it, but I would rather suffer
spiritual pain from insults people hurl against me,
in place of this physical pain.

Indeed I enjoy spiritual pain suffered for your sake;
*   and I happily embrace the disrespect of this world,*
*   so long as I am obeying your will.*
But in my feebleness, I cannot endure this present illness.
Save me from it.

ag Hammarskjold (1905-1961) was a Swedish economist, politician and the second Secretary General of the United Nations (1953-61). There his leadership greatly enhanced the prestige and effectiveness of the UN. He was posthumously awarded the Nobel Peace Prize in 1961. Although widely known for his diplomatic work, very few knew that Hammarskjold was one of the century's great mystics. "The greatest journey is the journey inward," he noted. For many years he privately wrote and kept a diary essentially devoted to the development of his own inner life. Those personal writings were discovered after his death and many were surprised by his spiritual awareness. Reading his *Markings,* it becomes clear that a private faith guided his public role. Sadly, on September 18, 1961, a plane crash in central Africa took his life. At the time he was attempting to negotiate a cease-fire between the government of the Congo and a secessionist group in Katanga. That mission was typical of his profound commitment to peace and his readiness to take on personal danger on behalf of a better world.

For a Humble Heart:

You *who are over us,*
You who are one of us,
You who are also within us,
May all see you in me also,
May I prepare the way for you,
May I thank you for all that shall fall to my lot,
May I also not forget the needs of others,
Keep me in your love

As you would that all should be kept in mine.
May everything in this my being be directed to your glory
And may I never despair.
  For I am under your hand,
  And in you is all power and goodness.

Give me a pure heart—that I may see you,
A humble heart—that I may hear you,
A heart of love—that I may serve you,
A heart of faith—that I may abide in you.
A love of life and men as God loves them—
  for the sake of their infinite possibilities,
    to wait like him
    to judge like him
    without passing judgment,
    to obey the order when it is given
    and never look back—
then he can use you—then, perhaps, he will use you.
And if he doesn't use you—what matter? In his hand,
  every moment has its meaning, its greatness, its glory,
  its peace, its co-inherence.

John Bunyan (1628-1688) observed that "in prayer it is better to have a heart without words, than words without a heart." Born into a home where his father was a tinker (a traveling mender of metal household utensils), Bunyan's formal education consisted of two years in elementary school. Then he pursued his father's trade. In his time that trade was regarded as humble and even frowned upon by most people. He married at twenty-one. Although his first wife's name is unknown, it is known that she brought to the marriage two religious books that belonged to her godly parents. Bunyan read those and experienced an awakening and curiosity about the spiritual life. In 1653 Bunyan joined a non-conformist (Puritan) congregation and in 1657 began preaching. During that time he began writing and publishing pamphlets.

In 1658 his wife and mother of their four children died. He married a second wife, Elizabeth, in 1659. A year later Bunyan was imprisoned when laws against non-conformist churches were revived. During that time it became illegal to conduct worship services except in accordance with Anglican ritual. Except for short periods, Bunyan spend the next twelve years in prison. Although he was heartbroken by being separated from his family and the ensuing poverty that his imprisonment brought them, he still declared from prison: "If you would let me out today, I should preach tomorrow!" He used his prison time to write more and longer works. It was while in prison he began writing his highly influential *Pilgrim's Progress*. That book has been translated into hundreds of languages. Bunyan died in poverty on August 31, 1688.

For Courage to Follow Christ:

O God, *we are grateful to you for letting*
your voice sound through the prophets and the saints
> *of the Bible.*
But most of all we pay you thanks for speaking your word
through Jesus Christ our Lord.
As we have heard your revelation in Him,
> *we pray for courage to 'follow him through*
> *heaven and hell, the earth, the sea, and the air.'*
In His name. Amen.

Prayer Before Meditating:

Eternal Companion, *from whose presence*
> *we have never been detached,*
> *we seek in our moments of meditation this day*
> *a share of your wisdom, power, and love.*
As we generously receive of your bountiful Spirit,
> *we turn with sympathy to our fellow men,*
> *trying to benefit their lives as you have*
> *benefited us in prayer.*
In the Redeemer's name. Amen.

Peter Abelard (1079-1142) lived a life filled with contradictions and tensions. He can be viewed as a saint or a sinner, a philosopher or a theologian, as an architect of Christian intellectualism or a dangerous heretic. After studying with many of the leading teachers of his day, Abelard began his own teaching career, first in Melun and Corbeil and later in Paris. A bold and original thinker, he drew large numbers of appreciative students to his lectures. Many of the greatest minds of the twelfth century were students of his, including Peter Lombard, as well as many future leaders of Christianity: several popes, twenty cardinals and nearly fifty bishops. While in Paris, Abelard lived with and was a guest of Fulbert, who was the canon at Notre Dame. Abelard fell in love with Fulbert's niece, Heloise, and a son was born to them. Abelard offered to marry her, but she chose to enter a convent instead, believing a marriage would hinder Abelard's career in the church. In retaliation, Fulbert ordered the castration of Abelard, who then entered the monastery of St. Denis. In spite of their separation, Abelard and Heloise continued a lifelong correspondence. Her published letters made them classic figures among the world's greatest lovers. After twenty years in the monastery, Abelard returned to Paris as a teacher where he encountered difficulties with church leaders because he believed that reason informed faith. Although some viewed him as laying a foundation for atheism, Abelard declared: "I do not want to be a philosopher if it means resisting St. Paul; I do not wish to be Aristotle if it must separate me from Christ." His writings on the Trinity eventually brought him into conflict with Bernard of Clairvaux. Abelard was condemned by both the French bishops and even the Pope. Peter of Cluny came to his defense, allowing him some level of freedom. He ended his days as a teacher at the Chalon-sur-Salone priory. His final resting place was with Heloise at the Pére Lachaise cemetery in Paris, a site that courting couples still frequent.

To Identify with the Suffering of Christ:

Lord, you go forth alone to your sacrifice.
You offer yourself to death, which you have come to destroy.
What can we miserable sinners plead,
*   who know that for the deeds that we have done, you atone?*
Ours is the guilt, Lord: why then must you suffer
*   torture for our sins?*
Make our hearts so to share in your Passion, that
*   our fellow-suffering may invite your mercy.*
This is the night of tears and the three days'
*   eventide of sadness, until the daybreak with*
*   the risen Christ and with joy to those that mourn.*
May we so suffer with you, Lord, that we may be partners
*   of your glory, and our three days' mourning shall*
*   pass away and become your Easter joy.*

Susannah Wesley (1669-1743) was the mother of John and Charles Wesley, founders of the Methodist Church. Her father Samuel was a prominent non-conformist minister, but she rejected non-conformist Christianity at thirteen years of age and joined the Church of England. In 1689 she married Samuel Wesley and bore him nineteen children, nine of whom died as infants. Both education and religious formation were methodically provided for the children by Susannah. The children were taught the Lord's Prayer as soon as they could speak and then recited it each morning and evening. All children spent six hours per day in school with lessons taught by their mother and father. In addition, at the beginning and close of every day each of the elder children took one of the younger and read them the psalm of the day and a chapter in the Bible. Her faith was intensely practical. "There are two things to do about the Gospel—believe it and behave it," she stated. Susannah's spirituality deeply impacted two of her sons in particular: John became a renowned preacher, and Charles wrote more than 6,000 hymns. Her prayers are intensely personal and practical.

For the Right Use of Disappointment:

Help me, *O Lord, to make a true use of all disappointments and calamities in this life, in such a way that they may unite my heart more closely with you. Cause them to separate my affections from worldly things and inspire my soul with more vigor in the pursuit of true happiness.*

For Confidence in God:

I thank you, *O God, for the relief and satisfaction of mind that come with firm assurance that you govern the world; for the patience and resignation to your providence that we are afforded as I reflect that even the tumultuous and irregular actions of the sinful are, nevertheless, under your direction, who are wise, good, and omnipotent, and have promised to make all things work together for good to those who love you.*

Richard Allen (1760-1831) was a founder of the African Methodist Episcopal church, one of America's most vigorous black denominations, and born a slave. Allen was converted at the age of seventeen by Methodist preachers. He immediately began to preach the gospel, first to his family, then to his master (who was also a convert), and finally to blacks and whites across America. Allen taught himself to read and write, and was eventually able to purchase his freedom. While working at various trades to support himself as a preacher, Allen made his way to Philadelphia at the age of twenty-six. With several other blacks he regularly worshipped at St. George's Methodist Church. Onc Sunday in 1787, while Allen's friend Absalom Jones was praying publicly, white trustees of the church forced him to his seat in an effort to silence him. Allen and the other blacks left the church and founded the Free African Society, America's first organization established by blacks for blacks. In 1799 Allen was ordained a Methodist minister, but because of growing race tensions within the denomination Allen and other black ministers organized their own church, the African Methodist Episcopal Church. Richard Allen became its first bishop in 1816.

Prayer of Faith:

I believe, *O God,*
that you are an eternal, incomprehensible spirit,
infinite in all perfections;
who did make all things out of nothing,
and do govern them all by your wise providence.

Let me always adore you with profound humility,
as my Sovereign Lord; and help me to love and praise
you with godlike affections and suitable devotion.

I believe, O Lord,
that you have not abandoned me
to the dim light of my own reason to conduct me to happiness,
but that you have revealed in the Holy Scriptures
whatever is necessary for me to believe and practice,
in order for my eternal salvation.

Prayer of Love:

O, crucified Jesus! *in whom I live,*
and without whom I die;
mortify in me all sensual desires;
inflame my heart with your holy love,
that I may no longer esteem the vanities of this world,
but place my affections entirely on you.
Let my last breath, when my soul shall leave my body,
breathe forth love to you, my God;
I entered into life without acknowledging you,
let me therefore finish it in loving you;
O let this last act of life be love,
remembering that God is love.

Brooke Foss Westcott (1825-1901) was highly regarded as a Christian intellectual, New Testament scholar, and a bishop in the Church of England. He attended Trinity College, Cambridge, where he became a fellow in 1849 and was ordained in 1851. He wrote numerous commentaries on New Testament books as well as the single most influential two-volume critical text of the New Testament in Greek, co-authored with his friend F. J. Hort. His commentaries on the book of Hebrews, John and the Epistles of John are considered classics. Wescott was popular with clergy and laity who often sought him out for spiritual and vocational advice. His wisdom is evident in this observation: "Temptation commonly comes through that for which we are naturally fitted." Wescott became president of the Cambridge Clergy Training School, now Westcott House. In 1890 he became Bishop of Durham. As a bishop he continued to publish books but also became involved with social issues of the day, especially the struggle of poor miners.

For Correction of Our Mistakes:

We ask you, *O God, the God of truth,*
That what we know not of things we ought to know
You will teach us.
That what we know of truth
You will keep us therein.
That what we are mistaken in, as men must be,
You will correct.
That at whatever things we stumble
You will yet establish us.
And from all things that are false
And from all knowledge that would be harmful,
You will evermore defend us,
Through Jesus Christ, our Lord.

To Love One Another:

Almighty God, *and most merciful Father,*
you have given us a new commandment that we
should love one another;
give us also grace that we may fulfill it.
Make us gentle, courteous and forebearing.
Direct our lives so that we may look each to the
good of the other in word and deed.
And hallow all our friendships by the blessing of your Spirit,
for his sake who loved us and gave himself for us,
Jesus Christ our lord.

acrina the Younger (c. 327-379) was a woman of considerable learning and spiritual influence. She was born in Cappadocian Caesarea and was the older sister of Basil the Great and Gregory of Nyssa. Engaged to be married at one point, she was devastated by the death of her fiance. Upon his death, she turned to religious life and founded a monastery on the family estate where she was joined by her mother Emelia and former slaves. Gregory wrote a biography of her life and attributed to her the role of an imaginary teacher in his classic *On the Soul and Resurrection.* By casting her into that role, he clearly showed the spiritual impact she had on his life and those around her.

For a Good Death:

O Lord, *you have taken from us the fear of death; you make*
the close of life the commencement of a new and truer life.
You wilt suffer our bodies to sleep,
and then will call us with the trumpet at the end of time.
Now send an angel of light beside me; have him take
my hand and lead me to the place of rest, where there is water
for my thirst beside the dwelling place of the Holy Fathers.

If in weakness of the flesh I have sinned in word, or deed, forgive sins on earth. When I am divested of my body, may I stand before you without faults or sins, in your own hands.

Anselm of Canterbury (1033-1109) experienced a major rift with his father over the matter of his career. His father wanted him to work in affairs of state and politics. Anselm chose to become a monk. In 1057 Anselm left home and traveled to Burgundy (France) for two years before settling into a Benedictine monastery at Bec, Normandy, where he studied under the renowned theologian Lanfranc. There Anselm took monastic vows and eventually became the Abbot of Bec (1078-1093). Anselm continued to teach and is often regarded as the most outstanding theologian between St. Augustine and St. Thomas Aquinas. While Abbot of Bec, Anselm journeyed three times to England where he impressed the English clergy with his teachings. Those same English clergy urged that Anselm be appointed Archbishop of Canterbury when the position became vacant. He was eventually appointed Archbishop in 1093. He died in office at nearly eighty years of age. Although highly trained and educated, Anselm was aware of the limitations of knowledge: "God often works more by the illiterate seeking the things that are God's than by the learned seeking the things that are their own."

For Those in Trouble and Distress:

We bring *before you the troubles and perils*
of people and nations,
the sighing of prisoners and captives,
the sorrows of the bereaved,
the necessities of strangers,
the helplessness of the weak,
the despondency of the weary,
the failing powers of the aged.

O Lord, draw near to each;
for the sake of Jesus Christ our Lord.

For a Greater Desire of God:

O Lord our God, *grant us grace*
to desire you
with our whole heart,
that so desiring we may seek and find you,
and so finding you, may love you,
and loving you, may hate those sins
from which you have redeemed us.

Mirabai (1498-1565) expresses the spirituality of
Bhaktism, a branch of Hinduism which stresses
devotion to a personal god and a desire for mystical union or oneness with that god. Mirabai is a
highly regarded poet and mystic. Her God,
whom she alternately refers to as Krishna and Hari (Lord), is manifested in her poems as her beloved or her true husband. Thus,
many of her poems and prayers actually have an erotic and passionate component to them, much like the Old Testament book
Song of Solomon. Her life story is a blending of fact and legend and
deals with her defiance of an earthly husband, of her miraculous
survival of attempts on her life by her husband and his family, and
of her running away to join a group of mystical devotees of Krishna.

For Increasing Perfection:

I am *thirsting for your love, my Beloved!*
I shall make this body a lamp,
and my tender heart shall be its wick;
I shall fill it with the scented oil of my young love
and burn it night and day at Your shrine, O Beloved!

For Your love I shall sacrifice all the wealth of my youth;
Your name shall be the crown of my head.
I am longing for You, O my Lord:
for the season of sowing has come;
but You are not beside me.
Clouds gather on my brows and my eyes shed heavy showers.
My parents gave me to You, I have become Yours forever;
who but You can be my Lord?
This separation troubles my breast; make me Your own;
make me perfect like You, O Lord of Perfection.

homas Aquinas (1225-1274) was unkindly labeled a "dumb Sicilian ox" because of his physical size and silence in the classroom. He would, however, emerge as a gifted theologian whose impact would last for centuries. He had great intellectual abilities and such intense concentration that he would dictate his thoughts to four secretaries at one time. His writings shaped the thinking of theologians for several generations. On December 6, 1272, he received a revelation from God. As a result of that experience he concluded: "The end of my labors is come. All that I have written appears to be so much as straw after the things that have been revealed to me." He stopped writing after that.

For a Steadfast Heart:

Give me, *O Lord, a steadfast heart,*
which no unworthy affection may drag downwards;
give me an unconquered heart,
which no tribulation can wear out;
give me an upright heart,
which no unworthy purpose may tempt aside.
Bestow on me also, O Lord my God,
understanding to know you,
diligence to seek you,

wisdom to find you,
and a faithfulness that may finally embrace you,
through Jesus Christ our Lord, Amen.

For Purity of Thought and Action in Daily Life:

𝕲rant, 𝕷ord, *that I may gladly share*
what I have with the needy,
humbly ask for what I need from him who has,
sincerely admit the evil I have done,
calmly bear the evil I suffer,
not envy my neighbor for his blessings,
and thank you unceasingly
whenever you hear my prayer.

echthild of Magdenburg (1210-1280) observed: "If you love the justice of Jesus Christ more than you fear human judgment, then you will seek to do compassion." Mechthild was a German mystic and writer born into a noble family in Saxony. She left home around 1230 to become a Beguine, a lay sister. Her community was devoted to prayer, poverty and service among the poor and sick. Toward the end of her life Mechthild entered the convent at Helfta, probably under pressure from church inquisitors who disapproved of the "unorthodox" spirituality of her writing as well as her criticisms of clerical corruption. As a contemplative she had visions which she was instructed to write down by her religious superior. Those writings were later published as *The Light of the Godhead* and had considerable influence in medieval Germany.

To Have the Faithfulness of a Dog:

𝕷ord, *since you have taken from me all that I had from you,*
yet of your grace leave me the gift which every dog has by nature:

that of being true to you in my distress,
when I am deprived of all consolation.
This I desire more fervently than your heavenly kingdom!

Prayer of Praise to the Mystery of God:

O burning *mountain, O chosen sun,*
O perfect moon, O fathomless well,
O unattainable height, O clearness beyond measure,
O wisdom without end, O mercy without limit,
O strength beyond resistance, O crown of all majesty,
The humblest you created sings your praise.

Robert Louis Stevenson (1850-1894) is one of the few novelists whose books, especially *Treasure Island* and *Dr. Jekyll and Mr. Hyde,* have stood the test of time and remain popular among both adults and children. This is a wonderful legacy considering the fact that Stevenson said of his writings: "My fame will not last more than four years." Born in Edinburgh, Scotland, Stevenson expected to follow his father's footsteps and become an engineer. He changed his studies to law, however. Chronically ill due to an unhealthy lung, Stevenson was advised to travel abroad in the hopes his lung condition would improve. During his wanderings he began to write travel books, essays and short stories, eventually turning to novels. Stevenson ultimately settled in Samoa with his wife and two children. Though he is best known for his books, Stevenson also wrote prayers, many of them for Samoan converts to Christianity.

For Strength and Loyalty:

Lord, bless us, *if it may be,*
in all our innocent endeavors.
If it may not, give us strength to encounter what is to come,
that we be brave in peril,

> constant in tribulation,
>> temperate in wrath and in all changes of fortune,
>> and, down to the gates of death, loyal and loving
>> to one another.
> As the clay to the potter,
>> as the windmill to the wind,
>> as children of their sire,
>> we beg of you this help and mercy for Christ's sake.

At Evening and for the New Day:

We resign *into your hands our sleeping bodies,*
> *our cold hearths and open doors.*
Give us to awaken with smiles;
> *give us to labor smiling.*
As the sun returns in the east,
> *so let our patience be renewed with dawn;*
> *as the sun lightens the world, so let our*
> *loving kindness make bright this house*
> *of our habitation.*

K arl Barth (1886-1968) once critiqued Christianity, declaring: "The church with no great anguish on its heart has no great music on its lips." Barth was a theologian of the Swiss Reformed Church whose theological reputation was established with his *Commentary on the Letter to the Romans* (1919). He pastored churches for twelve years before becoming a theology professor at Gottingen (1921-25). That chair was a new professorship established by the Reformed Church with money from the American Presbyterian Church. Barth later taught at Bonn (1930-35). With the rise of Hitler and the Nazi Party, Barth published a series of pamphlets opposing Hitler's perversion of the Christian faith. He was forced to leave the city and his position when he refused to take an unconditional oath to Hitler. Barth returned to his hometown of Basel, Switzerland, where he became a professor until his retirement in 1962. Barth continued teaching and writing to the end of his life. During the ten years before his retirement, Barth often preached to inmates in Basel's prison. Although regarded as a pivotal theologian of the twentieth century, Barth had a humble view of himself and his work: "When the day comes when I have to appear before my Lord, then I will not come with my deeds, with the volumes of my *Dogmatics* on my back. All the angels there would have to laugh. But then I shall also not say, 'I have always meant well; I had good faith.' No, then I will only say one thing: 'Lord, be merciful to me, a poor sinner!'"

When Standing Before God:

O Lord our God, *you know who we are;*
men with good consciences and with bad,
persons who are content and those who are discontent,
the certain and the uncertain,
Christians by conviction and by convention,
those who believe and those who half believe,
those who disbelieve.
But now we all stand before you, in all our differences,
yet alike in that we are all in the wrong with you
and with one another,
that we must all one day die,
that we would be lost without your grace,
but also in that your grace is promised
and made available to us
all in your dear Son, Jesus Christ.

An Easter Prayer:

O Lord God, *our Father. You are the light*
that can never be put out;
and now you give us a light that shall drive away all darkness.

You are love without coldness, and you have given us such
warmth in our hearts that we can love all when we meet.

You are the life that defies death, and you have opened for us
the way that leads to eternal life.

Do not let any of us remain apathetic or indifferent
   to the wondrous glory of Easter,
but let the light of our risen Lord
   reach every corner of our dull hearts.

Rabindranath Tagore (1861-1941) was the youngest of fourteen children born in Calcutta to Maharishi Devendranath Tagore, a great religious reformer in India. Rabindranath had a life-changing mystical experience when he was eighteen. At the time he was visiting his brother's family at their villa on the Ganges River. He describes what transpired: "One day while I stood watching at early dawn, the sun sending out its rays from behind the trees, I suddenly felt as if some ancient mist had in a moment lifted from my sight, and the morning light on the face of the world revealed an inner radiance of joy." The result of that mystical experience lingered with Rabindranath for four days, during which he lived in a state of heightened spiritual awareness. Ordinary images were infused with joy and delight—a man and a woman walking together, a mother playing with her child, two cows standing side by side. These rather ordinary events were, for Rabindranath, beautiful images of the divine presence in the world. Rabindranath gained worldwide fame as an Indian poet, philosopher, writer and mystic. He won the Nobel Prize for Literature in 1913. Although born into a family that practiced the Hindu religion, Rabindranath did not limit himself to Hinduism. He was drawn to aspects of Buddhism and embraced spiritual light wherever he encountered it. His spirituality drove him to work on behalf of the poor for the last fifty years of his life. Their plight became his personal cause.

To Never Disown the Poor:

This is my prayer *to you, my lord—*
strike, strike at the root of penury in my heart.
Give me the strength lightly to bear my joys and sorrows.
Give me the strength never to disown the poor
or bend my knees before insolent might.
Give me the strength to raise my mind high above daily trifles.
And give me the strength to surrender my strength
to your will and love.

Augustine of Hippo (354-430) once observed while speaking of the universal human search for God: "You have put salt in our mouths that we may thirst for you." The great teacher and preacher of the early church was born at Tagast in today's Algeria to a devout Christian mother and a father who did not practice the faith. Gifted with exceptional intellectual skills, Augustine was a brilliant student. He studied at the University of Carthage where he abandoned his faith and, in 372, took a mistress who remained with him for about thirteen years and bore him a son, Adeodatus (who died around 390). Much information is known about Augustine because of his writings, especially *Confessions* and *Retractions*. In 384 Augustine was appointed professor of rhetoric at a school in Milan, Italy. There his mother's prayers were answered, as Augustine came under the influence of Ambrose, Bishop of Milan. The bishop was a gifted preacher and his well planned and eloquently delivered sermons made a positive impact upon Augustine. He was baptized by Ambrose in 387. Within five years Augustine became a bishop in his native North Africa. Though written hundreds of years ago, Augustine's prayers continue to be popular and instructive.

For Dependence Upon God:

Lord, *what we know not, teach us.*

Lord, what we have not, give us.
Lord, what we are not, make us.

When Experiencing Trouble:

O God, *by your mercy strengthen us who lie exposed*
to the rough storms of troubles and temptations.
Help us against our own negligence and cowardice,
and defend us from the treachery of our unfaithful hearts.
Comfort us, we ask you, and bring us to your
safe haven of peace and happiness.

For Those Who Suffer:

Tend to *your sick ones, O Lord Christ;*
rest your weary ones;
bless your dying ones;
soothe your suffering ones;
shield your joyous ones;
and all for your love's sake.

Sun Bu-er (1124-?) was a married woman and mother of three children who became one of the most famous Taoist sages of her era. At the age of fifty-one she devoted herself full-time to the practice of Tao, or the Way. Followers of Tao believe the entire universe is filled with a mystical presence or an eternal principle which Lao-tzu called the Tao, a term usually translated as Way or Path, but which can also mean Teaching. The Tao is a great impersonal mystery or Absolute which can only be apprehended via the heart through silent meditations. The following prayer/poem dealing with worry and anxiety was composed by Sun Bu-er. Within her poem can be identified some classic aspects of Taoist spirituality: cyclical changes in the body are related to the cycles or seasons of the natural world, and the importance of allowing matters to evolve and take their course.

To Be in Harmony with the World:

There is *a body outside the body,*
Which has nothing do with anything produced by magical arts.
Making this aware energy completely pervasive
Is the living, active, unified, original spirit.
The bright moon congeals the gold liquid,
Blue lotus refines jade reality.
When you've cooked the marrow of the sun and moon,
The pearl is so bright you don't worry about poverty.

eresa of Calcutta (1910-1997) was one of the most inspiring persons of the twentieth century. She became known world-wide and was deeply respected by both Christians and non-Christians alike and was awarded the Nobel Peace Prize in 1979. She originally joined the Sisters of Loreto in 1928 at Rathfarnham, Ireland. There she expressed a desire and call to work in India. She was sent as a novice to study and minister in Darjeeling, and was assigned to teach at the Loreto school in Calcutta in 1928. By 1946 she became convinced God wanted more from her and felt increasingly called to serve the very poor. Two years later, with permission of her superior, she left the Loreto convent, took the name Teresa, and, dressed in a simple blue and white sari, went to live in a Calcutta slum area where she cared for the destitute and dying and taught the children of the very poorest. She was soon joined by others, including those whom she had taught. In 1950 the Missionaries of Charity was approved as a new religious order. "The biggest disease of today…is the feeling of being unwanted," she said. Treating that "disease" became the focus of all her work.

To Serve Those in Poverty and Hunger:

Make us worthy, *Lord, to serve our fellowmen*
throughout the world who live and die in poverty and hunger.

Give them, through our hands, this day their daily bread,
  and by our understanding love,
  give peace and joy.

To Spread Love:

O God *the Father of all, you ask every one of us to*
  spread love where the poor are humiliated,
  joy where the Church is brought low,
  and reconciliation where people are divided,
  father against son,
  mother against daughter,
  husband against wife,
  believers against those who cannot believe,
  Christians against their unloved fellow Christians.
You open this way for us,
  so that the wounded body of Jesus Christ, your Church,
  may be leaven of communion for the poor of the earth
  and in the whole human family.

artin Luther (1483-1546) rose from a humble birth as a miner's son to become a monk, scholar, professor and leader of the Protestant Reformation. Ordained a priest in 1507, Luther became a professor of Scripture at the University of Wittenberg, a post he held until his death. As a scripture scholar he developed the theology of human justification by faith in God alone. While critical of various aspects of church teaching, Luther was greatly angered by the sale of indulgences (an indulgence was the formal remission of temporal punishment for a sin) to help fund the rebuilding of St. Peter's church in Rome. In 1517 he posted his famed Ninety-Five Theses, which criticized indulgences, on the door of the castle church. He was excommunicated from the church and took refuge in Wartburg castle, where he began translating the Bible into German. Because of Luther's views, a reform movement of "Lutherans" spread quickly with congregations sprouting all over Germany. Luther promoted reformation rather than destruction of the church. Those reformations included: substituting a German service in place of the Latin Mass, proclamation of the Gospel by preaching, congregational hymn singing, and married clergy. Luther himself married a former nun, Katherine von Bora, in 1525. Prayer was always a vital part of Luther's life. "I am so busy now that if I did not spend two or three hours in prayer, I could not get through the day," he once said.

Prayer of Gratitude:

Lord God, *heavenly Father,*
we know that we are dear children of yours and that
you are our beloved Father, not because we deserve
it, nor could ever merit it, but because our dear Lord,
your only begotten Son, Jesus Christ, wills to be
our brother, and of his own accord offers and makes
this blessing known to us.
Since we may consider ourselves his brothers and sisters
and he regards us as such, you will permit us to become
and remain your children forever. Amen.

When Under Severe Criticism:

I would *prefer to have peaceful days and be out*
of this turmoil. But yours, O Lord, is this cause;
it is righteous and eternal.
Stand by me, you true Eternal God!
In no man do I trust.
Stand by me, O God, in the name of your dear Son,
Jesus Christ, who shall be my Defense and Shelter,
yes, my Mighty Fortress, through the might and strength
of your Holy Spirit. Amen.

Evelyn Underhill (1875-1941) enjoyed the honor of being the first woman invited to give a series of theological lectures at Oxford University in 1921. Yet Underhill was not a theologian nor even a professor of theology, but a mystic and writer of books on mysticism. Born in London to Sir Arthur Underhill, a distinguished lawyer, Underhill was educated at King's College for Women. Though an Anglican all her life, she was strongly drawn to Catholic spirituality. In 1911 she wrote the classic work *Mysticism: A Study in the Nature and Development of Man's Spiritual Consciousness.* Underhill wrote numerous other books on spiritual growth and development that were well received by both clergy and laity. Her writings make the mystical life accessible and even desirable for ordinary people. Consider, for example, her thought that all of us are called to be saints: "We may allow that saints are specialists; but they are specialists in a career to which all Christians are called. They have achieved, as it were, the classic status. They are the advance guard of the army; but we, after all, are marching in the main ranks. The whole army is dedicated to the same supernatural cause; and we ought to remember…that every one of us wears the same uniform as the saints, has access to the same privileges, is taught the same drill and fed with the same food. The difference between them and us is a difference in degree, not in kind."

To Recognize God:

Lord! *going out from this silence, teach me to be more alert,*
humble, expectant than I have been in the past:
ever ready to encounter you in quiet, homely ways:
In every appeal to my compassion, every act of unselfish love
which shows up and humbles my imperfect love,
may I recognize you: still walking through the world.
Give me that grace of simplicity
which alone can receive your mystery.
Come and abide with me!
Meet me, walk with me!
Enlighten my mind!

To Follow in the Paths of the Saints:

Your paths *are well-trodden.*
Along them you and your saints have carried
healing and love to ordinary men and women
where they are.
Teach me to serve them as you serve—
with patience,
simplicity,
reverence,
and love.
Your spirit is not given that we may escape
life's friction and demands,
but so that we may live the common life
as you would have it lived—
on earth as in heaven.

John Baillie (1886-1960) chaired an unusual committee during World War II. He served the Church of Scotland (Presbyterian) as chair person of a commission appointed "for the interpretation of the will of God in the present crisis." After his theological education, Baillie became a professor of theology in New York, Toronto, and finally Edinburgh University, where he taught until his retirement in 1956. A gifted teacher, students came to him from all over the world. Although his academic field was theology, Baillie is best known for his devotional classic *A Diary of Private Prayer* (1936). A keen observer of spiritual development, Baillie offered this critique of Christianity: "We may suspect, then, that the real reason why Christians are less distinguishable from the world than they used to be is not that there is more of the quality of holiness in the world, but that there is less of it in the Church."

To Rejoice in Creation:

Creator Spirit, *who broods everlastingly*

over the lands and waters of earth,
enduing them with forms and colours
  which no human skill can copy,
give me today, I ask you, the mind and heart
  to rejoice in your creation.

Prayer of Praise:

I praise you *for the life that stirs within me*
I praise you for the bright and beautiful world
  into which I go;
I praise you for the earth and sea and sky,
  for scudding cloud and singing bird;
I praise you for the work thou hast given me to do;
I praise you for all that thou hast given me
  to fill my leisure hours;
I praise you for my friends;
I praise you for music and books
  and good company and all pure pleasures.

Pierre Teilhard de Chardin (1881-1955) died in New York on Easter Sunday, April 10th, 1955. The Jesuit theologian and scientist was born in France and ordained into the Society of Jesus in 1911. A creative theologian, Teilhard de Chardin was strongly attracted to the natural sciences and studied geology and paleontology. He was a professor at the Catholic University of Paris from 1920 to 1928 and for many years worked to develop a synthesis between science and religion. Although his attempt to relate the Christian concept of creation to contemporary scientific understandings were considered unique and remarkable, Teilhard de Chardin was viewed with suspicion by church authorities. His Society of Jesus would not allow him to publish many of his writings nor was he permitted to accept a chair at the College of France because of his radical evolutionary views. In spite of this censure, he remained faithful to his church and his order.

For the Gift of Life:

In the life *which wells up in me*
and in the matter which sustains me,
I find much more than Your gifts. It is You Yourself whom I find,
*   You who makes me participate in Your being,*
*   You who molds me.*
Truly in the ruling and in the first disciplining
*   of my living strength,*
in the continually beneficent play of secondary causes, I touch,
as near as possible, the two faces of Your creative action, and I
encounter, and kiss, Your two marvelous hands—
*   the one which holds us so firmly that it is merged, in us,*
*   with the sources of life, and the other whose embrace is too*
*   wide that, at its slightest pressure, all the springs of the*
*   universe respond harmoniously together.*

To Be Purged of All Impurity:

Lord, *enfold me in the depth of your heart;*
and there hold me, refine, purge, and set me on fire,
raise me aloft, until my own self knows utter annihilation.

William Edward Burghardt Du Bois (1868-1963) became a legend in his own lifetime and is viewed as the single most influential African-American public intellectual of the twentieth century. He was simultaneously a scholar, professor, poet, novelist, historian, philosopher, journalist, author and human rights activist. He earned a B.A. from Fisk University in 1888 and was an honors graduate of Harvard in 1890. Six years later he was the first African-American to earn a Ph.D. from Harvard. He also studied at the University of Berlin between 1892 and 1894, gaining a broader intellectual and cultural experience from his extensive travels across Europe. A tireless and fearless leader, Du Bois launched the Niagara Movement in 1905 that advocated the immediate ending of racial discrimination and segregation. In 1909 he was one of the founders of the National Association for the Advancement of Colored People (NAACP). A decade later W. E. B. Du Bois organized the Pan-African Conferences in Paris with the hope of sensitizing world opinion to the conditions of blacks everywhere. Du Bois grew impatient with the NAACP's slow progress and late in his life renounced his U.S. citizenship. He died in Ghana one year before the Civil Rights Act of 1964. At the time of his death when he was ninety-five years old, Du Bois was still hard at work on a mammoth compendium of African culture titled *Encyclopedia Africana.*

For Grace:

Give us grace, *O God, to dare to do the deed*
which we well know cries to be done.

Let us not hesitate because of ease,
    or the words of men's mouths, or our own lives.
Mighty causes are calling us—
    the freeing of women,
    the training of children,
    the putting down of hate and murder and poverty—
all these and more.

But they call with voices that mean work and sacrifice and death.
Mercifully grant us, O God, the spirit of Esther that we say:
I will go unto the King and if I perish, I perish. Amen.

For Vision and Thought:

May God *deliver us from the curse of carelessness,*
    from thoughtless ill-considered deed.
The deliberate evil of the world, we know is great,
    but how much fortitude and strength and faith could we
    have to cure this and put it down, if only we were rid of
    the sickening discouraging mass of thoughtless careless acts

in men who know and mean better.

How willingly in all these years and now, have thousands of
mothers and fathers toiled and sweated and watched
from dawn till midnight over these children here,
only to be rewarded—not indeed by crime, but by persistent
carelessness almost worse than crime. The rules here are the
simple rules of work and growth. We do not make them—the
very circumstances of life make them. And when we break
them, it is not because we reason out their unreasonableness
but usually because we do not think—because of the lack of
Law and Order we are too lazy to see the weary pain-scarred
heart of the mother who sent us here. Give us vision and
thought. Amen.

John Wesley (1703-1791) was the fifteenth son of a British cleric. He was already actively involved in religious work when he experienced a spiritual awakening in which he felt his heart "strangely warmed." That was accompanied by an overwhelming sense of God's love that energized his spiritual life. He dedicated himself to spreading the gospel among those who were unchurched. At one point, Wesley prayed: "O Lord, let me not live to be useless!" That prayer was answered as Wesley traveled an average of 8,000 miles a year on horseback preaching to enormous crowds gathered in fields. "I regard the whole world as my parish," he declared. This unique approach to evangelism earned him ridicule and his adherents came to be mocked as "Methodists" because they were so methodical in their study and spiritual disciplines. Although Wesley hoped the Methodists would remain part of the Church of England, some of his own actions, particularly the ordinations he performed from 1784 on, broke ecclesiastical law and forced a separation. With the passing of time, active opposition to the Methodists lessened and eventually disappeared. At the time of his death, Wesley was described as "England's Grand Old Man." He remained an Anglican priest to the end. Although he frequently preached sermons on a daily basis, he was constantly preparing fresh, new material. "Once every seven years I burn all my sermons, for it is a shame if I cannot write better sermons now than I did seven years ago," he wrote. Today's many Methodist denominations and movements trace their origins to the remarkable ministry and life of John Wesley.

For Solid Footing:

Fix our steps, *O Lord, that we may not stagger*
at the uneven motions of the world,
but steadily go on to our glorious home,
neither censuring our journey by the weather we meet with,
nor turning out of the way by anything that befalls us.
Through Jesus Christ our Lord.

For Daily Guidance:

O Lord, *let nothing divert our advance towards you,*
but in this dangerous labyrinth of the world
and the whole course of our pilgrimage here,
your heavenly dictates be our map
and your holy life be our guide.

Elizabeth of Hungary (1207-1231) was an early social justice activist. She refused to eat any food which might be the fruit of injustice or exploitation. This Hungarian princess was born in Bratislava and at age four was betrothed to Prince Ludwig (age nine). Because this was a politically arranged relationship, Elizabeth's family sent her to live in the castle of her future husband. Despite the fact neither she nor Ludwig had any say in the matter, the two children developed a friendship that blossomed into a deep and loving marriage. While living at the castle, Elizabeth's style of life caused concern among her future in-laws. She dressed too simply, spent too much time in prayer, and was overly generous toward the poor, or so they said.

Ludwig objected fiercely when they suggested an alternative bride be found, declaring he would rather lose a mountain of gold than be separated from Elizabeth. They were married and quickly had three children. As princess she used her authority to establish several hospitals for the poor. In addition, she became the object of ridicule for personally nursing the sick and those with leprosy. When famine struck the kingdom she ordered the royal granaries opened to the poor. In 1227 Ludwig informed Elizabeth he had accepted command of a force of Crusaders bound for the Holy Land. Elizabeth feared for his safety. Several months later she learned Ludwig had died from the plague while on his journey. Without his protection, the royal family turned on Elizabeth and exiled her from the castle. Leaving with only her newborn child and what little she could carry, Elizabeth found herself living in a pig shed. Scandalized by her situation, relatives reluctantly provided her with a tiny cottage. Although she could have married again, she was resolved to remain single, devoting herself to prayer and service of the poor. In 1231—at the age of twenty-four—she fell ill and died. She was canonized by Pope Gregory IX a mere three years after her death.

When Grieving the Loss of a Spouse:

I have *lost everything.*
O my beloved brother,
  O friend of my heart,
  O my good and devout husband, you are dead,
  and have left me in misery!
How shall I live without you?
Ah, poor lonely widow and miserable woman that I am,
  may he who does not forsake widows and orphans
  console me.
O my God, console me!
O my Jesus, strengthen me in my weakness!

To Do God's Will:

As in heaven *your will is promptly performed,*
so may it be done on earth by all creatures,
particularly in me and by me.

A braham Lincoln (1809-1865) had to lead a nation that split shortly after he became President of the United States, plunging the country into a horrific civil war. "I have been driven many times to my knees by the over-whelming conviction that I had nowhere else to go," he said. "My own wisdom, and that of all about me, seemed insufficient for the day." Although he became a great leader of the United States, Lincoln's origins were extremely humble. He grew up on the frontier in pioneer surroundings, living in a log cabin. Schools were few and far between and teachers were scarce. Lincoln's entire education, which came via five different schools, amounted to less than twelve months of formal education. As a young adult, Lincoln read whatever books were available and self-educated himself in law sufficiently enough to become a lawyer. He practiced law in Illinois during the 1830s and 1840s and then became involved in politics. After several political wins and losses, Lincoln was elected president in 1860. During his presidency he often said: "My great concern is not whether God is on our side; my great concern is to be on God's side." As president of a nation at war with itself, Lincoln's prayers reflect the pressures he must have felt.

For a Nation at War:

Lord, *give us faith that right makes might.*
Grant, O merciful God, that with malice towards none,
with charity for all, with firmness in the right as you
give us to see the right, we may strive to finish the work
we are in; to bind up the nation's wounds,
to do all which may achieve a just and lasting peace

among ourselves and with all nations;
through Jesus Christ our Lord.

William Barclay (1907-1978) once described him-self, saying: "I have an essentially second-class mind." That humble assessment is remarkable, given the fact that Barclay's commentaries on the New Testament have sold millions of copies in English and have been translated into numerous languages. His clear and lucid explanation of New Testament books have been used by both clergy and laity. Barclay graduated from Glasgow University (1932), completed his graduate studies in Germany, and in 1933 became minister of a church made up almost entirely of people working in shipyards and factories. There he learned how to convey theological concepts in ways ordinary people could understand, while at the same time being careful not to patronize his audience. That skill would later translate itself into the more than fifty books he wrote, most of them extremely popular. Throughout his life, Barclay remained humble and resolute in his desire to be helpful to others.

To Be a Good Friend:

Help me, *O God, to be a good and a true friend:*
to be always loyal and never to let my friends down;
never to talk about them behind their backs
    in a way which I would not do before their faces;
never to betray a confidence or talk about the things
    which I ought to be silent;
always to be ready to share everything I have;
to be as true to my friends as I would wish them to be to me.
This I ask for the sake of him who is the greatest and truest of
all friends, for Jesus' sake.

eslie D. Weatherhead (1893-1976) was a pioneer in linking Christian spirituality with the insights of modern psychology. He once observed: "Perhaps we have done everything in the world to find health and radiance, happiness and peace, except to listen to, and heed the soul, crying always that same plaintive cry, the cry of the stream for the ocean, the cry of the prisoner for freedom, the cry of the watcher for morning, the cry of the wanderer for home, the cry of the starving for food, the cry of the soul for God." Born in London, he studied for the Methodist ministry. After several successful pastorates in the British Methodist Church, his gifts as a preacher and pastor were recognized when he was called in 1936 to be the minister of London City Temple, a Congregational church. Dr. Weatherhead was not only an exceptional preacher but a prolific author, writing more than thirty highly popular books.

For Those Who Share Their Healing Gifts:

We thank you *for every ministry of healing*
offered to those who suffer;
for the hospitals of our land and for all who staff them;
for the skill of doctors, surgeons and psychiatrists,
for dental surgeons, nurses, physiotherapists,
masseurs and technicians;
for the discovery of anesthetics and anodynes;
for curative drugs, for psychological methods,
and for every means of making people whole.
Show us how to prevent the burden of suffering
which weighs on so many lives,
that the humanity for which Christ died
may be indeed redeemed in body, mind and spirit.

For Those in Prison:

O Lord *God of justice, I lift up my heart in intercession for*
all those who are in prison. "Let the sighing of the prisoner come
before you." I cannot escape the truth that if sin were equated

*with crime, I too should be in prison. I have done things as evil
in your sight as the things that have brought others to prison,
with all the shame and disgrace to their dear ones as well as
to themselves.*

*Let this thought cleanse my heart of all false
superiority and all hypocrisy. Let it move me to
do anything in my power to comfort and to
uphold those who suffer through imprisonment.*

*Visit them in the lonely, bitter hours, and use their terrible
experience to win them to seek your forgiveness and to find
the comfort of the love that welcomes us all.*

Set them free in spirit now to turn to you.

*Deliver them from resentment and bring them back
to their loved ones and to the world of men, eager
to begin a new life.*

*Raise up those who will believe in them and help
them, and weave all their sadness into your plan for them.*

For Jesus Christ's sake. Amen

Basil the Great (330-379) developed the "Rule of St. Basil," which still continues today as the structure for monastic living in the Eastern Orthodox Church. Basil was born into one of the most remarkable Christian families. His grandmother Macrina, his father Basil, his mother Emilia, his sister Macrina, and his two younger brothers Gregory of Nyssa and Peter, bishop of Sebaste, were important leaders of Christianity and are all venerated as saints. The entire family had a noble reputation for ascetic piety, Christian charity, and for keeping an unwavering witness in spite of persecution. After receiving his education, Basil was briefly a teacher of rhetoric in 356. A year later he was baptized and became a hermit on his family's land. He became bishop of Caesarea in 370. While bishop he was engaged in many significant tasks, but two are often connected with his name: the establishment of monasticism as an integral part of church life, and defending and expanding the concept of the Trinity as basic to Christian theology. Perhaps because Basil spent time as a hermit he had an unusual sensitivity for God's creations.

To Enlarge Our Sense of Fellowship with Animals:

O God, *enlarge within us the sense of fellowship*
with all living things, our brothers the animals to whom
you gave the earth as their home in common with us.
We remember with shame that in the past we have exercised
the high dominion of man with ruthless cruelty so that
the voice of the earth, which should have gone up to you
in song, has been a groan of travail.
May we realize that they live not for us alone but for themselves
and for you, and they love the sweetness of life.

R obert Clarence Lawson (1883-1961) founded several Pentecostal denominations, including the Pentecostal Assemblies of the World and the Church of Our Lord Jesus Christ of the Apostolic Faith, with churches located mainly in St. Louis, Missouri, and San Antonio, Texas. A powerful preacher, he established the Refuge Church of Our Lord in New York City and in 1923, while still pastoring the church, began a New York radio broadcast that was widely and favorably received by African-American Christians. Uncommon to many Pentecostal preachers, Lawson's preaching stressed heavily the need for social, economic and political justice.

For Freedom from Prejudice:

O God, *who has made man in your own likeness,*

and who loves all whom you have made,
suffer us not because of difference of race, color, or condition
to separate ourselves from others and thereby from you;
but teach us the unity of your family
and the universality of your love.

As our Savior, as a Son, was born of a Hebrew
mother, who had the blood of many nations in her
veins; and ministered first to your family of the
Israelites, but rejoiced in the faith of a Syro-Phoenician
woman and of a Roman soldier, and suffered his cross
to be carried by an Ethiopian; teach us, also, while loving
and serving our own, to enter into the communion of the
whole family; and forbid that from pride of birth, color
or achievement and hardness of heart, we should despise
any for whom Christ died, or injure or grieve any in whom
he lives. We pray in Jesus' precious name. Amen.

Ludwig van Beethoven (1770-1827) lived a life filled with personal tragedy. He gradually became totally deaf, so that the major portion of his musically creative life was spent coping with that agonizing hardship. His musical genius was recognized early and at age seventeen he was sent to Vienna where he studied under Haydn. As a composer, Beethoven worked tirelessly in spite of his growing deafness. Although he exerted an enormous influence over secular music of the 19th century, his impact upon church music was quite limited. With the exception of the hymn "Joyful, Joyful We Adore Thee," very little of his other great works are used in church worship. Yet many feel that all of his music has a generic spirituality that speaks to those who are open to it.

For the Full Use of One's Talents for God:

O lead *my spirit,*
O raise it from these weary depths,

that ravished by your Art,
it may strive upwards with tempestuous fire.
For you alone have knowledge,
you alone can inspire enthusiasm.

To Be Fruitful in Good Works:

We must praise *your goodness that you have left*
   nothing undone to draw us to yourself.
But one thing we ask of you, our God,
   not to cease to work in our improvement.
Let us tend towards you, no matter by what means,
   and be fruitful in good works,
      for the sake of Jesus Christ our Lord.

Charles Albert Tindley (1851-1933) was a legendary preacher and leading African-American hymn writer in the Methodist Episcopal Church. Tindley was pastor of the East Calvary Methodist Church in Philadelphia, now renamed Tindley Memorial Methodist Episcopal Church. Although his church was huge, numbering some 5,000 members, it was his music that touched the lives of millions of African-American Christians, and ultimately white Christians as well. His hymns include "We'll Understand It Better By and By," "Stand By Me," and "Some Day." Tindley is regarded as a seminal figure in the founding of gospel music.

To Clean Up the World:

Help us *to witness, a witness for you, and be instruments in*
your hands so that people may know that you art through us
still redeeming the world. May folks, though us, find out you
art still in the business of saving men. May folks find out that
we have a relationship with Christ and that we have a vicarious
atonement, that can cleanse all sin.

*And help us to work with you, that through us you
shall do a mighty work. Clean up the world. Clear
out all the saloons everywhere. Wipe our flag clean
from all signs of war and may it be a signal of peace
and a new paradise everywhere that men may walk
and not be afraid.*

ope Benedict XV (1854-1922) urged President Woodrow
Wilson to use his great influence for a just peace in Europe, becoming the first pope to recognize the growing
power and authority of the United States. Born in Genoa,
Italy, he was elected to the Papacy in 1914 shortly after Europe plunged into the "war to end all wars." During the conflict,
Benedict worked hard to maintain neutrality, believing the Church
was better served when the papacy remained above political conflicts. He did, however, give and promote help for those ravaged by
war. As Pope, he is remembered as an opponent of "modernism"
and one who promoted the advancement of missions.

To Inspire World Leaders:

Inspire rulers *and people with counsels of meekness.
Heal the discords that tear nations asunder.*

*You who did shed your precious blood that they might
live as brothers, bring men together once more in loving
harmony. To the cry of the Apostle Peter: "Save us, Lord,
we perish," you did answer words of mercy and still the
raging waves. Deign now to hear our trustful prayers and
give back to the world order and peace.*

hich Nhat Hanh (1926-) knew he wanted to become a Buddhist monk when he was nine years old. Born in Vietnam, he became a monk at age sixteen and joined a Buddhist monastery. He quickly discovered, however, that monastic life and teaching was too far removed from the lives of everyday people to suit him. He shared his concerns with his teachers, but they failed to take him seriously. Thus he and some other monks left the monastery, establishing their own community at an abandoned temple in Saigon. There they studied Western philosophy and science with a goal of infusing the ancient teachings of Buddhism with contemporary principles, making them more attractive and accessible to a greater number of people. Nhat Hanh is frequently described as a Zen master, poet and peace advocate. In 1967 Martin Luther King, Jr. nominated him for the Nobel Peace Prize, declaring: "I do not personally know of anyone more worthy of the Nobel Peace Prize than this gentle monk from Vietnam."

Litany for Peace:

As we are *together, praying for Peace,*
let us truly be with each other.
(Silence)
Let us pay attention to our breathing.
(Silence)
Let us be relaxed in our bodies and our minds.
(Silence)
Let us be at peace with our bodies and our minds.
(Silence)
Let us return to ourselves and become wholly ourselves.
Let us maintain a half smile on our faces.
(Silence)
Let us be aware of the source of being common to us all
and to all living things.
(Silence)
Evoking the presence of the Great Compassion, let us fill our
hearts with our own compassion—toward ourselves and

towards all living beings.
(Silence)
*Let us pray that all living beings realize that they are all brothers
and sisters, all nourished from the same source of life.*
(Silence)
*Let us pray that we ourselves cease to be the cause of suffering
to each other.*
(Silence)
*Let us plead with ourselves to live in a way which will not
deprive other living beings of air, water, food, shelter or
the chance to live.*
(Silence)
*With humility, with awareness of the existence of life and of the
sufferings that are going on around us, let us pray for the
establishment of peace in our hearts and on earth.*
Amen.

oward Thurman (1900-1981) is frequently described as
the greatest African-American mystic of the twentieth
century. Ordained a Baptist minister, Thurman was
deeply influenced by the Quaker strain of thought. His
first pastorate was at the Mount Zion Baptist Church in
Oberlin, Ohio. Thurman then served as professor of religion and
director of religious life at Morehouse College and Spelman College and dean of Rankin Chapel at Howard University (1932-1944).
He was a co-founder in San Francisco of an integrated congregation—the Church for the Fellowship of All Peoples (1944-1953). In
1953 he accepted a call to become dean of the Daniel L. Marsh
Chapel at Boston University where he served until his retirement in
1965. Various religion editors for secular magazines and newspapers
cited Thurman as one of the greatest preachers of the twentieth
century. His influence continues to be felt through his various
books.

For Awareness of God's Perfect Timing:

I need *your sense of time.*
Always I have an underlying anxiety about things.
Sometimes I am in a hurry to achieve my ends
And am completely without patience.
It is hard for me to realize that some growth is slow,
That all processes are not swift. I cannot always discriminate
Between what takes time to develop and what can be rushed,
Because my sense of time is dulled.
I measure things in terms of happenings.
O to understand the meaning of perspective
That I may do all things with a profound sense of leisure
*   —of time.*

To Leave the Ego Behind:

My ego *is like a fortress.*
I have built its walls stone by stone
To hold out the invasion of the love of God.
But I have stayed here long enough.
There is light over the barriers, O my God—
The darkness of my house forgive
And overtake my soul.
I relax the barriers.
I abandon all that I think I am,
All that I hope to be,
All that I possess.

E ugene Bersier (1831-1889) was an influential pastor in the French Reformed Church. The Swiss native studied theology in Switzerland and Germany. He made a lengthy visit to America (1848-1850), returning to Paris where he became pastor of a congregation affiliated with the Free Reformed Church. His church was part of a group that broke away from the mainline Reformed Church of France. Concerned for greater unity among Christians, Bersier persuaded his congregation to rejoin the larger Reformed Church of France. He wrote books on worship and liturgy. It was, however, his published sermons that gained him a popular following across Europe. They were translated into Russian, Swedish, Danish, German and English.

For Deliverance from War in the Soul:

O you *who know our hearts,*
and who sees our temptations and struggles,
have pity upon us, and deliver us from the sins
which make war upon our souls.
You are all powerful, and we are weak and erring.
Our trust is in you, O faithful and good God.
Deliver us from the bondage of evil, and grant that
we may hereafter be thy devoted servants,
serving you in the freedom of holy love,
for Christ's sake.

For Strength to Complete Tasks:

O God, *from whom we have received life,*
and all earthly blessings,
give unto us each day what we need.
Give unto all of us strength to perform faithfully
our appointed tasks; bless the work of our hands
and of our minds.
Grant that we may ever serve you, in sickness and in health,
in necessity and in abundance;
sanctify our joys and our trials, and give us grace to seek first
your kingdom and its righteousness,
in the sure and certain faith
that all else shall be added unto us;
through Jesus Christ, thy Son, our Lord and Savior.

*T*eresa of Avila (1515-1582) hungered for a spiritual life and, despite her aristocratic father's objections, entered a convent when she was twenty. In 1555 she had a mystical experience of God which thoroughly transformed her. Because she was ridiculed for her visions, she founded a new convent with a stricter monastic rule at her birthplace in Avila, Spain. Called the "barefoot" Carmelites, Teresa's nuns wore coarse brown habits and sandals. They ate no meat and spent their days doing manual work. She often reminded people that God is always present in their lives. "We need no wings to go in search of Him," she said, "but have only to find a place where we can be alone—and look upon Him present within us." Her prayers have a remarkably practical element.

To Reduce Worry:

Let nothing *disturb you;*
let nothing dismay you;
all things pass:
God never changes.
Peace attains all it strives for.
He who has God finds he lacks nothing:
God alone suffices.

For Deliverance from "Sour-Faced Saints":

From silly *devotions*
and from sour-faced saints,
good Lord, deliver us.

*D*ietrich Bonhoeffer (1906-1945) was the son of professor Karl Bonhoeffer, the leading neurologist and psychiatrist teaching at the University of Berlin. Dietrich studied theology in Berlin and became a lecturer there in 1930. As early as 1933, Bonhoeffer was concerned about Hitler and the Nazi movement, even denouncing Nazi philosophy in a radio broadcast. In 1935, while an instructor at Berlin University, he wrote on behalf of the Jews saying: "Only he who cries our for the Jews may sing Gregorian chants." On November 9th, 1938, on Kristallnacht, when 7,500 Jewish shops were looted and 35,000 Jews were arrested, Bonheoffer underlined Psalm 74 verse 7 in his Bible: "They set your sanctuary on fire; they desecrated the dwelling place of your name, bringing it to the ground." While many clergy yielded to Hitler's interference in church matters, Bonhoeffer resisted and refused. He was part of a group that created the "confessing church" in Germany, a dedicated group of Christian men and women whose adherence was to God, not the state under Hitler. In 1935 Bonhoeffer began and led an "illegal" seminary in Ginkenwalde. He also identified himself with the resistance movement against Adolf Hitler. Bonhoeffer gradually moved from a pacifist position to the view that a dictator like Hitler could only be overthrown by force, and he involved himself in a plot to assassinate Hitler. Bonhoeffer was arrested in April 1943 and hung in 1944 by the Gestapo. "Bonhoeffer was one of the very few men I have ever met to whom his God was real and close," said an English officer imprisoned with him at Flossenburg in Bavaria. Bonhoeffer is one of Christianity's twentieth century martyrs.

While Awaiting Execution:

O God, *early in the morning I cry to you.*
Help me to pray and to concentrate my thoughts on you:
I cannot do this alone.
In me there is darkness,
But with you there is light;
I am lonely, but you do not leave me;
I am feeble in heart, but with you there is help;
I am restless, but with you there is peace.
In me there is bitterness, but with you there is patience;
I do not understand your ways,
But you know the way for me.

For Love that Blots Out All Hatred:

O Holy Spirit, *give me faith that will protect me
from despair, from passions, and from vice;
give me such love for God and men as will
blot out all hatred and bitterness;
give me the hope that will deliver me from fear
and faint-heartedness.*

John Knox (1513-1572) was trained as a notary. He was greatly influenced by the preaching of the Lutheran minister George Wishart in the mid-1540s and embraced the Protestant movement. He became leader of the reformation in Scotland but had to flee when Mary Tudor became the Roman Catholic Queen of England. Knox retreated to Geneva where he was profoundly influenced by the theology and Presbyterianism of John Calvin. When the political climate was more favorable, Knox returned to Scotland where he began to reform the Scottish Church along Calvinist lines. He acknowledged that he was in constant need of spiritual growth and maturity. He wrote, "In youth, in middle age, and now after many battles, I find nothing in me but corruption."

A Wedding Blessing:

The Lord *sanctify and bless you,
the Lord pour the riches of his grace upon you,
that you may please him
and live together in holy love
to your lives' end. So be it.*

Prayer for the Church:

O God *of all power, who has called from death
the great pastor of the sheep, our Lord Jesus:
comfort and defend the flock which has been redeemed*

by the blood of the eternal testament.
Increase the number of true preachers;
lighten the hearts of the ignorant;
relieve the pains of such as be afflicted,
especially of those that suffer for the testimony of the truth;
by the power of our Lord Jesus Christ.

F rancis Asbury (1745-1816) is regarded as the founder of the Methodist movement in America even though there were other Methodist preachers who preceded him to the New World. Born in England near Birmingham, his parents were early converts of Methodism's founder John Wesley. Their son Francis embraced the faith as his own when he was fourteen and began lay preaching at sixteen. In 1771 Wesley issued a call for volunteers to go to America as missionaries. Asbury eagerly responded. During the sea journey he recorded in his journal why he was making the perilous journey: "I am going to live for God, and bring others to do so." Arriving in the colonies, Asbury assumed leadership of the Methodist mission. There he differed with the prevailing view of the Methodist clergy. Those already in America favored stationed, or clergy settled in one location. Asbury felt that an itinerant or traveling clergy was better suited to the growing and expanding new nation. His own style set the tone as Asbury traveled some 270,000 miles, mostly on horseback, across the inhabited parts of America. He crossed the Allegheny Mountains more than sixty times, became a master woodsman of the American countryside, and came to be one of the best-known people in North America. "Go into every kitchen and shop; address all, aged and young, on the salvation of their souls," was his exhortation to Methodist preachers. Throughout his life, Asbury was a model of single-minded service to God and humanity: "My present mode of conduct is…to read about one hundred pages a day; usually to pray in public five times a day; to preach in the open air every other day; and to lecture in prayer meeting every evening." He ordained more than 4,000 preachers, and at the time of his death there were over

214,000 Methodists in the United States. One of the largest theological seminaries in the United States bears his name, Asbury Theological Seminary in Wilmore, Kentucky.

For Total Dependence on God:

Our Father, *we realize our dependence on you.*
When we are weak, then we are strong.
Afflictions may be our crosses,
> *but they can become crowns if we will sanctify them*
> *as is our privilege.*
Help us to take the sicknesses, the burdens,
> *the losses, the calamities,*
> *and use them as means of grace*
> *to center our afflictions on our Savior.*
> *Give me this kind of courage, this kind of faith.*
> *In Jesus' name.*

Johann Tauler (1300-1361) was a German Dominican mystic. He studied philosophy and theology in Cologne and Paris. He was highly regarded as a preacher and as a spiritual director of sisters in religious orders. Tauler was also noted for his complete devotion to those suffering from the Black Death. He never wrote, but his sermons were recorded by others and collected into a book titled *The Spiritual Conferences.* In one of his sermons he reminded listeners: "God has all power in heaven and earth, but the power to do his work in man against man's will he has not got."

For the Wise Use of Suffering:

May Jesus Christ, *the king of glory, help us to make*
the right use of all the suffering that comes to us and to offer
to him the incense of a patient and trustful heart;
for his name's sake. Amen.

Evangeline Cory Booth (1865-1950) literally spent her whole life in service of the Salvation Army. She was the daughter of William and Catherine Booth, founders of the organization. By age fifteen she was made a sergeant and at age twenty-three became principal of the Salvation Army's International Training College in London. Her abilities and energies were widely recognized. In 1896 she was appointed field commissioner for Canada and in 1904 became commander of Salvation Army operations in the United States. Her ministry culminated in 1934 when she was selected to be the fourth General of the Salvation Army, becoming the first woman to hold that position. A feminist ahead of her time, Booth once observed: "The forces of prejudice, of selfishness, of ignorance, which have arrested the progress and curtailed the influence of womankind for centuries, are receding from the foreground of the future, and with astonished vision we look upon the limitless fields of progress." Booth received many public honors including a Distinguished Service Medal conferred by President Woodrow Wilson in 1919.

To Receive Moral Strength:

Dear crucified Lord, *in the shadow of your cross
we may receive moral strength, that divine courage which will
enable us to combat the evils of selfishness, greed, indulgence
and all unworthiness that would prevent our deliberations
leading us to decisions for the highest good of the little village
as well as of the great city; for the poor and the nearly poor
as well as for the places of affluence; for those who are weak in
the face of temptation as well as for those who can stand strong.*

*Help us to remember, dear Savior, that we appear before
you as individuals, separate and alone. Be the captain
of our souls! Then if poverty comes we shall not be so poor,
and if sorrow comes we shall not be so sad, and if death comes*

we shall not be afraid. O God of all nations, Jesus Christ
the world's Redeemer, hear us as we pray, and have mercy
upon us, for Jesus' sake.

C lement I of Rome (died c. 100) is regarded as one of the earliest "apostolic fathers" and was the fourth Bishop of Rome, also known as the Pope. He wrote a letter to the church at Corinth around 96 A.D. that is among the earliest Christian writing outside of the New Testament. In that letter he quotes from the Old Testament and from the words of Jesus—using sayings found in Matthew, Mark and Luke. He also quotes from the book of Romans, I Corinthians, and Hebrews, thus providing important evidence that books which later became part of the New Testament were circulating among the churches by the end of the first century. His letter also refers to the martyrdom of the apostles Peter and Paul and references a mission of Paul to the "western boundary," meaning Spain.

For God's Help to All Who Are Hurting:

We beg you, *Lord, to help and defend us.*
Deliver the oppressed,
 pity the insignificant,
 raise the fallen,
 show yourself to the needy,
 heal the sick,
 bring back those of your people who have gone astray,
 feed the hungry,
 lift up the weak,
 take off the prisoners' chains.
May every nation come to know that you alone are God,
 that Jesus Christ is your Child,
 that we are your people,
 the sheep that you pasture.

To Be Grounded:

O God, *Almighty, Father of our Lord Jesus Christ,*
   grant us, we pray thee, to be grounded
   and settled in your truth by the coming down
   of the Holy Spirit into our hearts.
That which we know not, do reveal;
   that which is wanting in us, do fill up;
   that which we do know, do confirm;
   and keep us blameless in thy service,
   through the same Jesus Christ our Lord.

A nne Bradstreet (1612-1672) left England for the New World at the age of eighteen. Until then she led a leisurely and literate life. Learning to read and write, she had access to the finest works of her day—Spenser, Marlowe, Johnson, Herbert, Milton and Shakespeare. The two most important men in her life were Thomas Dudley, her father, and Simon Bradstreet, her husband. Both men were Puritans who pursued life in the New World as a religious conviction. Although opposed to their mission, Anne loved the two men and went to America with them. There she bore eight children, managed the household, and wrote poetry that reflected her spiritual awareness and evolution. She was the first poet to be published in America. Her writings reflect a practical spiritual wisdom. Consider these words: "There is no object that we see, no action that we do, no good that we enjoy, no evil that we feel or fear, but we may make some spiritual advantage of all; and he who makes such improvement is wise as well as pious."

To Remove Doubt:

Lord, *why should I doubt anymore, when you have given me such assurances of your love?*

First you are my creator, I your creature,
you my master, I your servant.

So wonderful are these thoughts that my spirit fails in me
at their consideration, and I am confounded to think that God,
who has done so much for me, should have so little from me.
But this is my comfort, that when I come to heaven, I shall
understand perfectly what he has done for me, and then I shall
be able to praise him as I ought. Lord, having this hope
let me purify myself as you are pure, and let me be no more afraid
of death, but even desire to be dissolved and be with you,
which is best of all.

Archibald Campbell Tait (1811-1882) was brought up a Presbyterian, but after attending Glasgow University (1827-1830) he decided to enter the ministry of the Church of England. He earned a scholarship to Oxford, where he distinguished himself academically. As bishop of London, he was instrumental in promoting effective preaching. At his urging, Westminster Abbey and St. Paul's Cathedral both began to hold popular preaching services Sunday evenings. In February 1869, he was consecrated Archbishop of Canterbury. Archbishop Tait was not immune to the tragedies of his day, however, and between March 11 and April 8, 1856, he and his wife lost five of their six daughters through scarlet fever. His prayer is powerful in its affirmation of God's goodness in the presence of great pain.

When a Child Has Died:

O God, *you have dealt very mysteriously with us.*
We have been passing through deep waters;
> *our feet were well-nigh gone, but though you slay us, yet will*
> *we trust in you....*
They are gone from us....You have reclaimed the lent jewels.

Yet, O Lord, shall I not thank you for now?
I will thank you not only for the children you have left to us,
but for those you have reclaimed.
I thank you for the blessing of the last ten years,
and for all the sweet memories of these lives.
I thank you for the full assurance that each has gone
to the arms of the Good Shepherd,
whom each loved according to the capacity of her years.
I thank you for the bright hopes of a happy reunion,
when we shall meet to part no more.
O Lord, for Jesus Christ's sake, comfort our desolate hearts.
May we be a united family in heart through the communion of
saints;
through Jesus Christ our Lord.

John Calvin (1509-1564) is generally recognized as a seminal figure in the development of Western culture. The Protestant reformer was born in France to a prosperous family who made certain he received the best education available. When he was fourteen, Calvin was enrolled at the University of Paris. Upon completing a Master of Arts degree, his father instructed him to leave his theological studies and begin a study of law. Dutifully, the son went to Orleans, where France's best law faculty was located. There he proved to be a brilliant student and earned a doctorate in law. His heart lay with theology, however, and he abandoned law after his father's death in 1531. Sometime between 1532 and early 1534, Calvin experienced a religious conversion that led him to embrace the emerging Protestant movement. By 1536 he completed and published the first edition of the *Institutes of the Christian Religion,* his famous compendium of Protestant theology. Persecution forced Calvin to flee to Basel. Eventually he settled in Geneva where he worked with the city council to turn the city into a model Christian community. By the time of his death, Calvin had considerable political and religious power in Geneva. His theological impact was felt all over Europe and the British Isles.

Before Studying Scripture:

O Lord, *heavenly Father, in whom is the fullness of light*
and wisdom, enlighten our minds by your Holy Spirit,
and give us grace to receive your Word with reverence
and humility, without which no one can understand
your truth. For Christ's sake, Amen.

For Sound Sleep and God's Mercy:

O merciful God, *temper our sleep*
that it be not disorderly,
that we may remain spotless both in body and soul,
yea that our sleep itself may be to your glory.

And although we have not passed this day without
greatly sinning against you, we ask you to hide our sins
with your mercy, as you hide all things on earth with
the darkness of the night, that we may not be cast out
from thy presence.

Relieve and comfort all those who are afflicted in mind,
body or estate. Through Jesus Christ our Lord.

Jonathan Edwards (1703-1758) was one of the most influential and controversial figures in American church history. Born in Connecticut, Edwards entered Yale University in 1716 when he was thirteen. Upon graduation, he remained at Yale where he studied for the ministry. In 1726 he was asked to minister at a Congregational church in Northampton, Massachusetts, a church pastored by his grandfather. Under the influence of Edwards' preaching, his church and many in the surrounding area experienced a religious revival in 1734-35. This spiritual awakening occurred again in 1739 but impacted a larger group of churches and came to be called the "Great Awakening." Although Edwards was regarded as one of the country's greatest preachers and theological thinkers, some of his views were unpopular and controversial. After a lengthy dispute with some in his church, the congregation voted to dismiss Edwards in 1750. The following year he settled in Stockbridge, Massachusetts, where he led a small church and served as teacher and missionary to Housatonnoc Indians living in the area. In 1758 he was persuaded to become president of the College of New Jersey (later renamed Princeton University). He died one month later (March 22) from smallpox. The following prayer was written on the occasion of the death of his friend, the missionary David Brainerd. Edwards' prayer at the funeral commends Brainerd's dedicated service.

To Be More Spiritually Engaged with the World:

Oh that *the things which were seen and heard in this extraordinary person; his holiness, heavenliness, labor and self-denial in life; his so remarkably devoting himself and his all, in heart and practice, to the glory of God; and the wonderful frame of mind manifested, in so steadfast a manner, under the expectation of death, and under the pains and agonies which brought it on; may excite in us all, both ministers and people, a due sense of the greatness of the work which we have to do in the world, of the excellency and amiableness of thorough religion in experience and practice, of the blessedness of the end of those whose death finishes such a life, and of the infinite value of their eternal reward, and effectually stir us up to constant endeavors that, in the way of such a holy life, we may at last come to a blessed an end. Amen.*

enry Martyn (1781-1812) was a prize-winning student at St. John's College, Cambridge, where he earned an M.A. in 1804 and a B.D. (Bachelor of Divinity) in 1805. A gifted linguist, he offered himself for service as a mission worker with the newly-formed Church Missionary Society but was turned down. He instead traveled to India as a chaplain with the East India Company. There he translated scripture into Urdu, Arabic and Persian. Sometime in 1810 he was advised to take a sea voyage to improve his health. He went to Persia where he continued his translation work. His Persian translation of the New Testament was presented to the Shah. Martyn died in Turkey before he returned to England, where he had hoped to marry Lydia Greenfell. While ill, Martyn was nursed and eventually buried by Christians connected to the Armenian Church.

For God's Help:

Lord, *I am blind and helpless,*
stupid and ignorant.
Cause me to hear;
cause me to know;
teach me to do;
lead me.

Prayer of Dedication:

Now *may the Spirit,*
who gave the Word,
and called me, I trust,
to be an interpreter of it,
graciously and powerfully
apply it to the hearts of sinners.

Thomas Cranmer (1489-1556) was an intellectual giant in his day. A person of immense learning, his personal library was larger than that of Cambridge University. He could read Latin, Greek, Hebrew, French, Italian and German. Cranmer found favor with Henry VIII by providing intellectual and theological support for the King's divorce campaign. In 1532 Henry rewarded Cranmer for his support by making him Archbishop of Canterbury. As Archbishop, Cranmer ordered that an English translation of the Bible should be placed in every church and read aloud regularly. He was also instrumental in transforming the Church of England when he compiled *The Book of Common Prayer* published in 1549. It translated the complex medieval Latin services into the language of the people. *The Book of Common Prayer* also helped shift congregants from being merely onlookers to participants in worship. He was arrested and executed when Mary Tudor ascended to the throne. His prayers are still used in Anglican and Episcopal prayer books today.

For Judges and Magistrates:

O heavenly Father, *at whose hand the weak shall take*
no wrong nor the mighty escape just judgment;
pour your grace upon your servants our judges and magistrates,
that by their true, fruitful and diligent execution
of justice to all equally,
you may be glorified, the commonwealth daily promoted,
and all live in peace and quietness, godliness and virtue;
through Jesus Christ our Lord.

For the Season of Lent:

Almighty *and everlasting God,*
you hate nothing that you have made,
and forgive the sins of all those who are penitent.
Create and make in us new and contrite hearts,
that, lamenting our sins
and acknowledging our wretchedness,

we may receive from you, the God of all mercy,
perfect forgiveness and peace;
through Jesus Christ our Lord. Amen.

Helder Pessoa Camara (1909-1999) was an outspoken prophetic voice for the poor of the world, especially those in South America. He was ordained a priest in 1931 and became archbishop of Olinda and Recife in his native Brazil. Camara used his office to speak and work on behalf of the poor. Brazilian authorities objected to his speaking and writing, and from 1968 to 1977 his activities were restricted by the military government. Camara's simplicity, charity, clarity of vision and courage of his convictions gained him international respect. He was awarded numerous peace prizes and was given honorary doctorates by universities in America, France and Germany.

Reflecting on Life's Blessings:

The *milk-float,*
the poor man begging,
the staircase and the lift,
the railway lines, the furrows of the sea,
the pedigree dog and the ownerless dog,
the pregnant woman,
the paper-boy,
the man who sweeps the streets,
the church, the school,
the office and the factory,
streets being widened,
hills being laid low,
the outward and the homeward road,
the key I used to open my front door;
whether sleeping or waking—
All, all, all
make me think of you.

What can I give to the Lord
for all he has given me?

hillip Melanchthon (1497-1560) wrote: "Unless you know
why Christ put on flesh and was nailed to the cross, what
good will it do you to know merely the history about
him?" Melanchthon was the son of George Scharzerd.
Phillip was given the name 'Melanchthon' (the Greek
equivalent of his name) by his great-uncle John Reuchlin, a prominent Hebrew scholar, because of Phillip's early interest in Greek. He
earned a B.A. at the age of fourteen and received an M.A. from Tub-
ingen the following year. By 1518 he established himself as a professor of Greek at Wittenberg University. There he developed a
close friendship with Martin Luther and published Luther's first
edition of influential lectures on the New Testament book of Romans. Although supportive of Luther and his reforms,
Melanchthon disliked conflict and controversy. Thus, he tried to
mediate between Catholics and Protestants, working hard to reconcile views between the two groups.

For the Unity of the Church:

To you, *O Son of God, Lord Jesus Christ,*
as you pray to the eternal Father, we pray,
make us one in him. Lighten our personal distress
and that of our society. Receive us into the
fellowship of those who believe. Turn our hearts,
O Christ, to everlasting truth and healing harmony.

O God, we do not desire new contentions and discord.
We pray only that the Son of God, our Lord Jesus Christ,
who for us died and rose from the grave, will guide us,
that all of us who are in many churches
and many communions may be one Church,
one Communion and one in him.

Amy Carmichael (1868-1951) was one of seven children born into a devout Presbyterian family in Northern Ireland. While in her twenties she went to India as a missionary with the Church of England. She served there for fifty-six years without ever taking a furlough. The children of India, especially those who were neglected and mistreated, became the focus of her efforts. In 1901 she founded the Dohnavur Fellowship, which cared for more than 1,000 children and operated three homes, a hospital, as well as engaging in evangelistic work. A deeply compassionate woman, she often said: "You can give without loving, but you cannot love without giving." Carmichael was a prolific writer, producing thirty-five books.

For Conformity to the Will of God:

Holy *Spirit*
think through me
till your ideas
are my ideas.

For Remembrance of God's Proximity:

It is not *far to go*
for you are near.
It is not far to go,
for you are here.
And not by traveling, Lord,
men come to you,
but by the way of love,
and we love you.

ohn Donne (1571-1631) was born into a Roman Catholic family at a time when anti-Catholic sentiments were at their highest in England. In spite of being a Catholic, Donne was able to attend Oxford and Cambridge Universities where he studied (but never practiced) law. In his younger years, Donne evidently had a weakness for women. His "profane" poems describe a number of mistresses. After struggling to find faith, Donne was ordained into the Church of England, rising rapidly to become dean of St. Paul's Cathedral in 1621. He is considered both a great poet and preacher. His sermons make up ten volumes. His book, *Devotions Upon Emergent Occasions* (1624) contains a famous passage that begins "No man is an island," and ends, "Ask not for whom the bell tolls; it tolls for thee."

To Be Used by God in Spite of Faults:

O eternal *God,*
let me, in spite of me,
be of so much use to your glory,
that by your mercy to my sin,
other sinners may see how much sin you can pardon.

Prayer of Need:

O Lord, *never suffer us to think*
that we can stand by ourselves,
and not need you.

For Everlasting Life:

Bring us, *O Lord God, at our last awakening*
into the house and gate of heaven,
to enter into that gate and dwell in that house,
where there shall be no darkness nor dazzling,
but one equal light;
no noise nor silence,
but one equal music;

no fears nor hopes,
    but one equal possession;
no ends nor beginnings,
    but one equal eternity
in the habitations of your glory and dominion,
    world without end.

harles Haddon Spurgeon (1834-1892) is noteworthy in that he was the most popular preacher of his day, consistently attracting crowds numbering in the thousands Sunday after Sunday. Because he was also a prolific author, his influence extended beyond England and into Europe and America. The son of a Congregational minister, Spurgeon was born at Kelvedon, Essex. As a teenager he chose to be baptized and joined a Baptist church. Experiencing a call to ministry, he served briefly at a small church before being called to the Baptist church in Southwark, London. The congregation was quite small when he arrived, but within weeks he was attracting large crowds, even though he was only twenty years old. A decision was quickly made to expand the church, but before long even the new building became too small to hold the congregation. As a result, the Metropolitan Tabernacle was erected at a cost of thirty-one thousand pounds and could seat six thousand people. Spurgeon preached there until shortly before his death. Spurgeon described his ministry this way: "Some are dead; you must rouse them. Some are troubled; you must comfort them. Others are burdened; you must point them to the burden-bearer. Still more are puzzled; you must enlighten them. Still others are careless and indifferent; you must warn and woo them."

For Spiritual Education:

Lord, *educate us for a higher life,*
    and let that life be begun here.
May we be always in the school, always disciples, and when we

are out in the world may we be trying to put into practice what
we have learned at Jesus' feet. What he tells us in darkness
may we proclaim in the light, and what he whispers in our ear
in the closets may we sound forth upon the housetops.

For Laughter and Singing:

Come and *help us, Lord Jesus.*
A vision of your face will brighten us;
  but to feel your Spirit touching us will make us vigorous.
Oh! for the leaping and walking of the man born lame.
May we today dance with holy joy,
  like David before the ark of God.
May a holy exhilaration take possession of every part of us;
  may we be glad in the Lord, may our mouth be filled with
  laughter, and our tongue with singing,
  "for the Lord has done great things for us and we are glad."

Catherine of Siena (1347-1386) chose her religious vocation at the age of sixteen. Born Caterina di Diacomo di Benincasa in Siena, the twenty-fourth of twenty-five children, Catherine practiced contemplation in solitude throughout her youth. She entered a Dominican order when she was eighteen. As a Dominican lay sister, she led a strict ascetic life. She emerged as a mystic activist, serving the poor, the sick and the dying during the plague as well as sharing in the poverty of the people. Catherine facilitated peace between the city states of Italy and the papacy. Some scholars credit her with the Pope's return from Avignon to Rome. Her fame as a woman with rare spiritual wisdom spread so widely that she was often consulted for important matters of state and the negotiation of treaties. She frequently advised people: "Build yourself a cell in your heart and retire there to pray." Although completely illiterate, she dictated prayers, letters and a book. A highly regarded mystic, she was declared a patron saint of Italy in 1939.

For Remembrance of God's Love:

𝔇𝔢𝔞𝔯 𝔏𝔬𝔯𝔡, *it seems that you are so madly in love*
with your creatures that you could not live without us.
So you created us; and then, when we turned away from you,
you redeemed us.

Yet you are God, and so have no need of us.
Your greatness is made no greater by our creation;
your power is made no stronger by our redemption.
You have no duty to care for us, no debt to repay us.
It is love, and love alone, which moves you.

wight L. Moody (1837-1899) said "the Christian on his knees sees more than the philosopher on tiptoe." The man who was to become the most famous American evangelist of the nineteenth century was forced to leave school at thirteen in order to work in his hometown of Northfield, Massachusetts. At seventeen he relocated to Boston where he converted and attended a Congregational Sunday school. In 1856 he moved to Chicago, where he experienced considerable financial success as a shoe salesman. Moody, however, had a great concern for the spiritual needs of youths and in 1860 abandoned his secular career to work full-time with the YMCA evangelizing young men. He also established a Sunday School for poor children, a non-denominational church, and a Bible Institute. While engaged in religious work, Moody met musician Ira D. Sankey. The two teamed up with Moody as evangelist and Sankey as musical director. Initially, Moody and Sankey had limited success, but gradually their evangelistic campaigns became popular across American and in England. During his lifetime Moody is believed to have covered a million miles on preaching tours and spoken to over 100 million people.

To Be Used by God:

Use me, *my Savior, for whatever purpose, and in whatever*
way, you may require.
Here is my poor heart, an empty vessel;
fill it with your grace.
Here is my sinful and troubled soul; quicken it and refresh
it with your love.
Take my heart for your abode; my mouth to spread the glory
of your name; my love and all my powers,
for the advancement of your believing people;
and never suffer the steadfastness and confidence
of my faith to abate;
so that at all times I may be enabled from the heart to say,
'Jesus needs me, and I him.'

Henry Sloan Coffin (1877-1954) was born in New York City
and educated at Yale, Edinburgh, and Union Theological
Seminary. He was ordained in 1900 and established a
Presbyterian mission in the Bronx. From 1905 to 1926 he
was pastor of Madison Avenue Presbyterian Church
where he became known as one of the finest preachers in the country. During that time he also taught practical theology at Union Theological Seminary and in 1926 became a professor and president of
that institution. His prayers reflect his mutual vocations, that of pastor and theological educator:

To Experience a Deeper Revelation of God:

Almighty *and ever-living God,*
you are beyond the grasp of our highest thought,
but within the reach of our frailest trust:

Come in the beauty of the morning's light
and reveal yourself to us.

Enrich us out of the heritage of seers and scholars and saints
into whose faith and labors we have entered,
and quicken us to new insights for our time;
that we may be possessors of the truth of many yesterdays,
partakers of your thoughts for today,
and creators with you of a better tomorrow;
through Jesus Christ, the Lord of the ages.

Thomas More (1478-1535) was a scholar, lawyer, politician and diplomat who served in the royal office as Lord Chancellor of England. Between 1499 and 1503 he went through a deep spiritual experience that impacted his life from then on. His refusal to support the divorce of King Henry VIII and to acknowledge the King as head of the church resulted in his imprisonment and eventual execution. "I am the King's good servant," he said, "but God's first." That final declaration led to his execution. More was a man with a great sense of humor. Even on the scaffold he showed his cheerful personality, saying to the executioner: "Assist me up. Coming down I can shift for myself."

For a Sense of Humor:

Lord, *grant me a holy heart*
that sees always what is fine and pure
and is not frightened at the sight of sin,
but creates order wherever it goes.
Grant me a heart that knows nothing of boredom,
weeping and sighing.
Let me not be too concerned with the bothersome thing
I call 'myself'.
Lord, give me a sense of humor,
and I will find happiness in life and profit for others.

iles Coverdale (1488-1568) was an Augustinian monk who became a supporter of the Reformation movement. He was born in York and educated at Cambridge University, earning degrees in philosophy and theology. Ordained to the priesthood in 1514, he soon joined the Augustinian monastery in Cambridge. Coverdale preached against the religious abuses of the day and consequently faced opposition that forced his departure from England for mainland Europe. There he began translating the Bible, eventually producing the first complete English Bible in 1535. (Tyndale had published the first English translation of the Greek New Testament in 1525). Coverdale's Bible, initially smuggled into England, became very popular and was eventually published by English printers under the protection of Thomas Cromwell. When the political climate changed, Coverdale returned to England, where he spent the rest of his days in the London area.

When Persecuted:

O God, *grant us patience when the wicked hurt us.*
O how impatient and angry we are when we think ourselves
unjustly slandered, reviled and hurt!
Christ suffers strokes upon his cheek, the innocent for the guilty;
yet we may not abide one rough word for his sake.
O Lord, grant us virtue and patience, power and strength,
that we may take all adversity with good will,
and with a gentle mind overcome it.
And if necessity and your honor require us to speak,
grant that we may do so with meekness and patience,
that the truth and your glory may be defended,
and our patience and steadfast continuance perceived.

For Christ to Remember Us:

O Jesus, *be mindful of your promise; think of us,*
your servants; and when we shall depart hence, speak
to our soul these loving words:
"Today you shall be with me in joy."

O Lord Jesus Christ, remember us your servants
who trust in you, when our tongues cannot speak,
when the sight of our eyes fails, and when our ears
are stopped. Let our soul always rejoice in you
and be joyful about your salvation, which you through
your death have purchased for us.

F rancis of Assisi (1181-1226) is perhaps the most popular and well-known saint in the world. Initially, Francis worked with his father, a wealthy cloth merchant. At twenty years of age he left home to join the military, where he was taken prisoner. He spent several months in confinement, during which he reflected on his life. Upon his release, he made a pilgrimage to Rome before returning home. While praying in the ruined church of San Damiano in Assisi he heard a voice instruct him: "Go and repair my house." Responding immediately, Francis sold off some of his father's cloth and gave the money to the church priest for repairs. Convinced that Francis was insane, his infuriated father denounced him and Francis began his life as the *povercello*, the little poor man. In fact, Francis regarded himself as "married to Lady Poverty." Although he did not intend to establish a religious order, a diverse group of men and women sought him out. Those individuals soon made up the community that came to be called "Franciscans." Francis died at the relatively young age of forty-five, his body worn out by his ascetic lifestyle. Left behind are many legends and stories about Francis, as well as many beautiful prayers.

Prayer of St. Francis:

Lord, *make me an instrument of your peace;*
Where there is hatred, let me sow love;
Where there is injury, pardon;
Where there is discord, union;
Where there is doubt, faith;
Where there is darkness, light;
Where there is sadness, joy.

O Divine Master, grant that I may not so much seek
To be consoled as to console;
To be understood as to understand;
To be loved as to love;
For it is in giving that we receive;
It is in pardoning that we are pardoned;
And it is in dying that we are born to eternal life.

Litany of Praise to God:

You are holy, Lord, the only God,
and your deeds are wonderful.
You are strong, you are great,
You are the most high, you are almighty.
You, Holy Father, are King of heaven and earth.
You are Three and One, Lord God, all good.
You are good, all good, supreme good, Lord God, living and true.
You are love, you are wisdom.
You are humility, you are endurance.
You are rest, you are peace.
You are joy and gladness, you are justice and moderation.
You are all our riches, and you suffice for us.
You are beauty, you are gentleness.
You are our protector, you are our guardian and defender.
You are courage, you are our haven and hope.
You are our faith, our great consolation.
You are our eternal life, great and wonderful Lord,
God almighty, merciful Savior.

Desiderius Erasmus (c. 1466-1536) was a Dutch scholar and the first modern translator of the New Testament. He was born a priest's son out of wedlock and consequently never had a normal family life. He was educated under the auspices of the Brethren of the Common Life, a popular order at the time that produced some of the fifteenth century's best teachers. In 1486, under pressure from his guardians, Erasmus entered an Augustinian monastery. His six years of study there resulted in a love of classical literature and thought. He was ordained in 1493, becoming the Latin secretary to the bishop of Cambrai, France. The bishop, noting Erasmus' considerable intellectual skills, allowed him to pursue theological studies in Paris. There he developed a permanent dislike for dogmatic theologians and their intolerance and hostility towards new ways of thinking. Erasmus studied further in Italy and England, where he taught Greek and divinity at Cambridge. Eventually he settled in Basel, Switzerland, where he prepared his Greek edition of the New Testament. Erasmus was outspoken in his criticisms of corruption in the Catholic Church. Although he saw the need for a reformation (which indeed followed), Erasmus remained a Catholic. He once critiqued the preachers of his day, saying: "If elephants can be trained to dance, lions to play, and leopards to hunt, surely preachers can be taught to preach."

To Be Empty:

Sever me *from myself that I may be grateful to you;*
may I perish to myself that I may be safe in you;
may I die to myself that I may live in you;
may I wither to myself that I may blossom in you;
may I be emptied of myself that I may abound in you;
may I be nothing to myself that I may be all to you.

For Christ's Guidance:

O Lord *Jesus Christ,*
you are the Way, the Truth, and the Life.
We pray you allow us never to stray from you,
who are the Way, nor distrust you, who are the Truth,
nor to rest in any one other thing than you, who are the Life.
Teach us, by your Holy Spirit, what to believe, what to do,
and how to take our rest.

Christina Rossetti (1830-1894) began writing as a teenager, becoming one of the most popular poets of her time. While she wrote poems for children and poems of love, a large aspect of her writing was spiritual. A deeply religious woman, she broke off one engagement and refused another offer of marriage because neither of the men shared her faith. Her piety is revealed through these words: "Were there no God, we would be in this glorious world with grateful hearts, and no one to thank."

When Weary and Burdened by Life:

O Lord *Jesus Christ,*
who art as the shadow of a great rock in a weary land,
who behold your weak creatures weary of labor,
weary of pleasure, weary of hope deferred, weary of self;
in your abundant compassion, and fellow feeling with us,
and unutterable tenderness, bring us, we pray,
unto your rest.

For Openness to God:

Open wide *the window of our spirits, O Lord,*
and fill us full of light;
open wide the door of our hearts, that we may receive
and entertain you with all our powers of adoration and love.

Siddhartha Gautama (c. 563-483 BC) is best known as "Buddha," which means enlightened one. When people refer to the Buddha, they usually mean the historical person named Sidhartha Gautama who lived in northern India, on the borders of Nepal. Gautama was born into a life of great luxury and was insulated from the knowledge of suffering. At the age of twenty-nine, however, he encountered aging, sickness and death. This caused him to reject his hedonistic lifestyle and venture out into the world to seek the truth about life. He renounced all wealth, becoming an ascetic. For six years he practiced a rigorous asceticism that included fasting and meditation. He came to the conclusion that both indulgence and austerity were inappropriate, and that a moderate lifestyle was more ideal. Still searching, Gautama decided to sit down under a tree for meditation. He vowed not to leave the site until he came to a realization of the ultimate truth. There he experienced his enlightenment, which reportedly involved the following: a recollection of all his previous lives, the ability to see the working of *karma* (action) in the lives of all beings, the complete destruction of ignorance and selfishness, and the attainment of nirvana—perfect peace, perfect knowledge, ultimate truth. Of course, his enlightenment was so profound that it was not easy to put his spiritual insights into words. He spent forty-five years teaching many followers. Gautama established a *sangha*, an order of monks and nuns, to help preserve and spread his teachings. He is said to have passed away peacefully at the age of eighty.

The Buddha's Blessing:

ꓐow may every living thing,
  young or old,
  weak or strong,
  living near or far,
  known or unknown,
  living or departed or yet unborn,
may every living thing be full of bliss.

lizabeth Fry (1780-1845) founded the Association for the Improvement of the Female Prisoners in Newgate (1817) and became Britain's leading prison reformer. Born to devout Quaker parents, Fry experienced a great spiritual awakening during a sermon by an American Quaker, William Savery. In 1800 she married Joseph Fry, a prosperous Quaker who gave her strong support as she began ministering to the poor. Fry gave medicine and clothing to the needy, encouraged parents to send their children to school, advocated Bible study, and organized libraries in more than five hundred coastguard stations around Britain. Her passion, however, was to improve the lot of prisoners. She became concerned about prison conditions in 1813 and began a ministry to female prisoners in Newgate jail. Through her association, she offered female prisoners education, paid employment and religious instruction. Fry campaigned widely in both Britain and Europe for prison reform. After touring prisons and making extensive notes, Fry her gave testimony in the House of Commons about conditions and the need for reform. Her influence extended beyond England, reaching Italy, Denmark and Russia. Of her lifelong call to service, she wrote: "Since my heart was touched at seventeen years old, I believe I never have awakened from sleep, in sickness or in health, by day or by night, without my first waking thought being, 'how best I might serve my Lord.'"

For Charitable Feelings Toward All:

O Lord, *may I be directed what to do*
   and what to leave undone,
and then may I humbly trust that a blessing will be with me
   in my various engagements.
Enable me, O Lord, to feel tenderly and charitably
   toward all my beloved fellow mortals.
Help me to have no soreness or improper feelings toward any.
Let me think no evil, bear all things,
   hope all things, endure all things.
Let me walk in all humility and Godly fear before all men
   and into your sight.

Reinhold Niebuhr (1892-1971) was minister of Bethel Evangelical Church in Detroit for thirteen years before becoming a professor at Union Theological Seminary in New York City in 1928. While he wrote several notable books, his broadest appeal to the general public came through a prayer attributed to him, commonly referred to as the "Serenity Prayer." That brief prayer has become tremendously popular because it contains practical wisdom reminding us not to waste valuable emotional energy battling with events that cannot be altered. The "Serenity Prayer" helps us to cope with the trials of our day and to focus on improving conditions during difficult times.

Serenity Prayer:

God grant me—
The serenity to accept the things I cannot change,
The courage to change the things I can,
And the wisdom to distinguish the one from the other.

For Pride in Our Labor:

Grant us grace, our Father,
to do our work this day as workers who need not be ashamed.
Give us the spirit of diligence and honest inquiry in our
quest for the spirit of charity in all our dealings with our
fellows, and the spirit of gaiety, courage, and a quiet mind in
facing all tasks and responsibilities.

Thomas Fuller (1608-1661) supported himself primarily through writing theology and church history. The English theologian and church historian published a number of notable works including *History of the Holy War*—a book chronicling the Christian Crusades (1639)—and his most celebrated work, *Church History of Britain* (1656). Although he published many books on church history, his rapid writing and quick research brought on the criticism that his material was somewhat "careless." Fuller fared better among critics when he wrote theology. He holds an important place among British writers of the seventeenth century for his works *Good Thoughts in Bad Times* (1645) and *Good Thoughts in Worse Times* (1647). For a time, Fuller served as chaplain to various members of the royal family. His writings contain many proverbs including: "Prayer should be the key of the day and the lock of the night."

To Learn the Art of Patience:

𝕷𝖔𝖗𝖉, *teach me the art of patience whilst I am well, and give me the use of it when I am sick. In that day either lighten my burden or strengthen my back.*

For Freedom from Envy:

𝕷𝖔𝖗𝖉, *I perceive my soul deeply guilty of envy. I would prefer your work not done than done by someone other than myself. Dispossess me, Lord, of this bad spirit, and turn my envy into holy emulation; yes, make other people's gifts to be mine, by making me thankful to you for them.*

Richard of Chichester (1197-1253) has rightly been described as "a model diocesan bishop." This godly man was born into a poor farm family. Although he worked long hours in the fields, he made time to study, eventually entering Oxford University. There he was so poor that he had to share a college gown and one warm tunic with two friends who all took turns wearing the garments when attending lectures. Richard's intellect and spiritually did not go unnoticed, and he was appointed bishop of Chichester. The king, however, refused to provide him with the material benefits that normally went with the post. Richard chose to share housing with a parish priest. He grew figs, visited his diocese on foot, wore simple clothing, ate only vegetarian food, and gave most of his money to the poor.

To Know God Better:

Thanks *be to thee, Lord Jesus Christ,*
for all the benefits which you have won for us,
for all the pains and insults which thou has borne for us.
O most merciful Redeemer, Friend and Brother,
may we know you more clearly,
love you more dearly,
and follow you more nearly,
day by day.

George Herbert (1593-1633) enjoyed a flourishing career as a teacher and professor until a series of deaths in 1624 deprived him of his influential patrons, including the King of England. An Anglican priest and poet, he was born in Montgomery, Wales, to a noble family. By 1630 he resolved to live and work as a simple parish priest and accepted an offer to be vicar of the Bemerton village church. He impressed local villagers by his consistent and careful pastoral care of the flock to which he was assigned. While at Bemerton he wrote many religious poems, many of which have been described as magnificent. Some of them were set to music and sung as hymns in the church. *A Priest to the Temple,* his small book offering pastoral guidance for country clergy, was published posthumously in 1652.

For a Grateful Heart:

You *have given so much to us,*
give us one thing more: a grateful heart.

To See God in All Things:

Teach me, *my God and King,*
In all things thee to see,
And what I do in anything,
To do it as for you!
All may of you partake,
Nothing can be so mean,
Which with this tincture (for your sake)
Will not grow bright and clean.
A servant with this clause
Makes drudgery divine!
Who sweeps a room as for your laws
Makes that and the action fine.

ildegard of Bingen (1098-1179) had mystical experiences as a child. Her first such visions came when she was about three years old. Not understanding them, she was often embarrassed and confused by the experiences, becoming reluctant to speak of them. In later life, however, she was persuaded to put her experiences into writing. Before doing so, she first obtained permission from both her archbishop as well as the Pope. A remarkably talented woman, Hildegard was a saint, abbess, author, musician and German mystic. Born to nobility in the diocese of Mainz, her parents were able to provide her with a sound education at a Benedictine convent. She eventually entered that order and spent the rest of her life with it. Her written revelations are contained in the book *Scivias*, regarded as a classic of medieval mysticism. Important church leaders were favorably impressed by her writing, including the Pope, who regarded her as a prophetess, and Bernard of Clairvaux, with whom she carried on a lifelong correspondence. Unlike many other mystics of the Middle Ages, Hildegard did not practice in isolation nor did she demonstrate an ascetic piety. In fact, she carried on an extensive correspondence, went on preaching tours, and her Benedictine monastery had indoor plumbing and served delicious food.

To Slay the Dragon Within:

(Ŋost *strong God, who is able to fight against you?*
I want you to help me fight against the flaming
  dragon of sin within me, that eats away my very soul.
I want to have the strongest sword in my hand,
  fashioned by you, with the sharpest blade that will
  cut through the dragon's scales.
And when I have slayed the dragon within myself,
  I want to offer a safe refuge for all who, like me,
  are frail and vulnerable. I will give them a sword
  to slay their own dragons, so that together we may
  live in joy and peace.

Walter Rauschenbusch (1861-1918) lived most of his life in Rochester, New York. He was born there, attended college and seminary there, and taught for the last twenty-one years of his life at the Rochester Baptist Theological Seminary. His one lengthy excursion from Rochester, however, provided him with experiences that changed his life. In 1886 Rauschenbusch became pastor of the Second German Baptist Church near Hell's Kitchen, a notorious slum area in New York City. As he ministered, he was deeply moved and concerned over the situation of poor immigrants and the socially disadvantaged. He saw first-hand the immigrants' sordid living conditions, labor exploitation by industrial giants, and governmental indifference to the suffering of the poor. That experience led to a personal transformation for Rauschenbusch. Looking back at what happened to him, Rauschenbusch wrote these words in 1913: "I began to work in New York and there, among the working people...I began to understand the connection between religious and social questions." He became well-known through his many writings and was called the "father of the social gospel in America." President Roosevelt consulted with Rauschenbusch to shape the Democratic Party's social policies. His prayers reflect his deep social concerns.

Grace over a Meal:

Our Father, *you are the final source of all our comforts and to you we give thanks for this food.*

But we also remember in gratitude the many men and women whose labor was necessary to produce it and who gathered it from the land and afar from the sea for our sustenance. Grant that they too may enjoy the fruit of their labor without want, and may be bound up with us in a fellowship of thankful hearts.

For the City and Nation:

O God, *grant us a vision of this city, fair as it might be:*
a city of justice, where none shall prey upon the other;
a city of plenty, where vice and poverty shall cease to fester;
a city of brotherhood, where success is founded on service,
*   and honor is given to the nobleness alone;*
a city of peace, where order shall not rest on force,
*   but on the love of all for each and all.*

Etty Hillesum (1914-1943) is often considered to be the "mystic of the Holocaust," as revealed by her carefully written journal notes kept while she was imprisoned in a Nazi concentration camp. Those journal entries have been described as a "testimony of faith, hope, and love, written in hell itself." She was born into a prosperous family of Dutch Jews who lived in Amsterdam. Most of the journal entries were made between 1941 and 1943 and were posthumously published under the title *An Interrupted Life: The Diaries of Etty Hillesum, 1941-1943.* The journal ends abruptly in September 1943 when Hillesum was moved to Auschwitz where she was murdered. In spite of living under the most extreme and horrific conditions, Hillesum was filled with awe, wonder and praise to God.

Prayer of Gratitude:

You *have made me so rich, O God, please let me share out Your beauty with open hands. My life has become an uninterrupted dialogue with You, O God, one great dialogue. Sometimes when I stand in some corner of the camp, my feet planted on Your earth, my eyes raised towards Your Heaven, tears sometimes run down my face, tears of deep emotion and gratitude.*

Rabi'a (717-801) was acknowledged in her preeminence above other Islamic Sufi teachers. Her status was remarkable given the rigid patriarchy that characterizes much of Middle Eastern life. According to her twelfth-century biographer Attar, Rabi'a is Islam's most important mystic: "That one set apart in the seclusion of holiness, that woman . . . on fire with love and longing…that woman who lost herself in union with the Divine, that one accepted by men as a second Mary." Rabi'a was born in Basra, orphaned, sold into slavery and later freed. Like the Christian Mary, many legends and myths have evolved around Rabi'a. One of those claims that when she prayed, her head was surrounded by light, much like a halo. That light is called *sakina* in Arabic and is similar to the Hebrew *shekhina*, the cloud of holiness indicating the presence of God. Rabi'a taught that love was the core of mystical union and she promoted a heavenly bridegroom, rejecting earthly marriage. Thus, many of her prayers are simply loving conversations with God.

Praise to God:

O **Lord,** *the stars are shining and the eyes of men are closed, and kings have shut their doors and every lover is alone with his beloved, and here am I alone with Thee.*

Blessings on Enemies:

Whatever share of this world Thou dost bestow on me,
bestow it on Thy enemies,
and whatever share of the next world Thou dost give me,
give to Thy friends. Thou art enough for me!

ulia Ward Howe (1819-1910) continues to be remembered for her most popular writing, *The Battle Hymn of the Republic.* She pursued studies in law and literature, receiving a doctorate of law from Tufts and Smith Colleges, as well as a doctorate of letters from Brown University. In 1843 she married the philanthropist and social reformer Samuel Gridley Howe. They lived in Boston and raised a family of six children. Howe was active in the Unitarian Church, often speaking in congregations throughout New England. An ardent opponent of slavery, she and her husband edited the Boston *Commonwealth,* a vigorous anti-slavery periodical (1851-1853). Howe also campaigned for child welfare, prison reform and equal education. A prolific writer, she published volumes of poetry, drama, biography and travel.

For the Patience of Saints:

O you, whose gifts are beyond words, you in whose loving
Fatherhood we are content to abide, help us to know that
You are near us today, and every day of our life on earth.

Give us, we pray, that faith in the conquering of good
deeds and purposes which may enable us to contend
successfully against the infirmities and temptations to which
our nature is subject.

May a sense of the true values of life keep us in the faith
appointed for us. May we seek the patience of your saints
and the wisdom of your prophets.

Florence Nightingale (1820-1910) was thirty-six when an illness forced her to leave her nursing station near the front lines of the Crimean War. Upon her return home, Nightingale received accolades from around the world: the Sultan of Turkey sent her a diamond bracelet, England's Prince Albert gave her the gift of a brooch, American poet Longfellow wrote a poem about her, medals of honor were given to her from France, Germany, Norway and England. The English nurse and hospital reformer was born in Florence, Italy, on May 12th. Committed to nursing at an early age—against her parents' wishes—Nightingale not only worked as a nurse but carefully studied advances in hygiene. She spent eleven years traveling abroad, visiting hospitals in Europe run by Protestant and Catholic sisterhoods. In 1853 she became superintendent of a London hospital for women. A year later the Crimean War broke out and Nightingale offered her services. She arrived with two friends and thirty-eight nurses. There Nightingale organized the barracks, sanitized the hospital, and cleaned up medical facilities at the front lines. Because of her firm discipline and adherence to sanitation principles, Nightingale's actions greatly reduced the mortality rate. Although the illness that forced Nightingale to return to England left her in a weakened condition for the rest of her life, she nevertheless continued to work at improving the nursing profession.

Prayer of Service to God:

O God, *you put into my heart this great desire*
to devote myself to the sick and sorrowful;
I offer it to you. Do with it what is for your service.

gnatius of Loyola (1491-1556) was born into a wealthy and powerful family living in the province of Guipuzcoa, Spain. As a child he lived in luxury and ease. That lifestyle came to an abrupt end when Spain and France battled over territory. Loyola, who was in the Spanish army, was seriously wounded in the leg by a cannon ball and had to undergo painful surgery and a lengthy recovery. During that time Loyola read several devotional books and experienced mystical visions of Christ and the Virgin Mary. His former interests in military honor were transformed into spiritual desires to serve God. As his calling took shape, Loyola envisioned companies of men—not knights—but soldiers of Christ. Eventually he established the Jesuit order, one which became more influential in the Catholic church than their numbers would suggest. Those who joined the Jesuit order were expected to share in the deep commitment and convictions of their founder. Examples of that commitment are found in many of Ignatius' prayers.

To Do God's Will:

Dearest *Lord, teach me to be generous;*
Teach me to serve you as you deserve;
To give and not to count the cost,
To fight and not to heed the wounds,
To toil and not to seek for rest,
To labor and not to seek reward,
Save that of knowing that I do your will.

To Be Used Completely by God:

Take, *Lord, all my liberty. Receive my memory,*
my understanding and my whole will.
Whatever I have and possess, you have given to me;
to you I restore it wholly, and to your will
I utterly surrender it for your direction.
Give me the love of you only,
with your grace, and I am rich enough;
nor ask I anything beside.

Charles Kingsley (1819-1875) has been described as a "muscular Christian" because he celebrated the values of being cheerful and robust. Kingsley was a British novelist, historian and priest of the Anglican Church. While serving as a minister he published tracts urging Christian socialism. The tracts emphasized the plight of the poor and working class. Although Kingsley was the author, he published them under the name "Pastor Lot." His concern for the poor reached a wider audience through his novels *Yeast* (1848) and *Alton Locke* (1850). Kingsley served as a chaplain to Queen Victoria and was professor of modern history at Cambridge. An ardent anti-Catholic, Kingsley engaged in debate with John Henry Newman, the country's leading Catholic. Kingsley extolled the benefits of activity: "Thank God every morning when you get up that you have something which must be done whether you like it or not," he wrote. "Being forced to work and forced to do your best will breed in you temperance, self-control, diligence, strength of will, content, and a hundred other virtues which the idle never know."

To Offer Ourselves to God:

Stir us up *to offer to you, O Lord,*
our bodies, our souls, our spirits,
in all we love and all we learn,
in all we plan and all we do,
to offer our labours, our pleasures, our sorrows to you;
to work through them for your Kingdom,
to live as those who are not their own,
but bought with your blood,
fed with your body;
yours from our birth-hour, yours now,
and yours for ever and ever.

To Remove Pride and Vanity:

O God, *grant that looking upon the face of the Lord,*
as into a glass, we may be changed into his likeness,
from glory to glory.

Take out of us all pride and vanity,
boasting and forwardness;
and give us the true courage which shows itself by gentleness;
the true wisdom which shows itself by simplicity;
and the true power which shows itself by modesty.

Julian of Norwich (c. 1342-c.1413) lived a solitary life of prayer and meditation. Almost nothing is known about her except what she wrote in her autobiographical book *Revelations of Divine Love*. Reliable tradition associates her with St. Julian's Church, Norwich, near which she lived out her life as a solitary contemplative. Her fame rests on her book, which she wrote in 1391. Julian says she received fifteen revelations from God one day in 1373 and another on the following day. In those visions she saw the sufferings of Christ. She meditated and reflected on those visions for twenty years, placing her focus on the love of God which, she believed, supplied the answer to all of life's problems, particularly the problem of evil in the world. "Peace and love are always alive in us, but we are not always alive to peace and love," Julian wrote. She summed up her doctrine of God in these words: "I saw three properties: the first is, that God made it. The second is, that God loveth it. The third is, that God keepeth it. But what beheld I therein? Verily the Maker, the Keeper, the Lover."

For More of God:

God, *of your goodness, give me yourself;*
for you are sufficient for me. I cannot properly
ask anything less, to be worthy of you.

If I were to ask less, I should always be in want.
In you alone do I have all.

John Oxenham (1852-1941) was the pen name of British novelist and poet William Dunkerley. After graduating from Victoria University in Manchester, he lived in France representing his father's business interests. He returned to England where he took up writing full-time. He penned more than forty novels and during World War I was one of England's most popular writers. His 1913 work, *Bees in Amber,* was rejected by publishers who felt it would not be a commercial success. Oxenham published it himself and, to his great surprise, watched it sell nearly a quarter million copies. In addition to writing, he was also an expert mountain climber. Oxenham served as a deacon and teacher at the Euling Congregational Church in London. He also wrote several hymns, including *In Christ There Is No East or West.*

Be with Me, Lord:

Through *every minute of this day,*
Be with me, Lord!
Through every day of all this week
Be with me, Lord!
Through every week of all this year
Be with me, Lord!
Through all the years of all this life,
Be with me, Lord!
So shall the days and weeks and years
Be threaded on a golden cord.
And all draw on with sweet accord
Unto your fullness, Lord,
That so, when time is past,
By grace I may at last,
Be with you, Lord.

Thomas à Kempis (1380-1471) wrote what may be the most widely read Christian book ever written, *The Imitation of Christ*. He lived in the fourteenth century when religious renewal was taking place in Europe. Part of that trend included translating the Bible into the vernacular and encouraging more involvement of laity in the life of the church. In Germany those were important issues for a community called The Brethren of the Common Life. Thomas Hemerken from Kempen, near Cologne, better knows as Thomas à Kempis, was educated by that community. He entered the order as a lay brother in 1399, becoming a monk in 1406. Thomas spent his time copying manuscripts, preaching and writing. Thomas exhibited a practical and fervent spirituality as revealed in these insights of his: "Never be entirely idle; but either be reading, or writing, or praying, or meditating, or endeavoring something for the public good;" and "Truly at the day of judgment we shall not be examined on what we have read, but what we have done; not how well we have spoken, but how religiously we have lived."

For Discernment:

Grant me, *O Lord, to know what is worth knowing,*
to love what is worth loving,
to praise what delights you most,
to value what is precious in your sight,
to hate what is offensive to you.

Do not let me judge by what I see,
nor pass sentence according to what I hear,
but to judge rightly between things that differ,
and above all to search out and to do what pleases you,
through Jesus Christ our Lord.

Blaise Pascal (1623-1662) was a French mathematician, philosopher and mystic. His brilliance was recognized while he was a child. When he was three Pascal's mother died, leaving him and two sisters in the care of their father. In 1631 his father moved his family to Paris where the elder Pascal could provide better cultural and educational opportunities for his children. By the time Pascal was twelve, he had worked out the equivalent of many of Euclid's geometrical theorems and subsequently made original contributions to geometry and calculus. At age seventeen, he had created one of the world's first calculating machines, a forerunner to future business machines and modern computers. He is credited with discovering "Pascal's Law," a principle of water pressure which formed the basis of modern hydraulics. In November 1654, Pascal experienced a mystical vision in which he discovered "the God of Abraham, the God of Isaac, the God of Jacob, and not of philosophers and men of science." One of his arguments for the existence of God was stated this way: "Let us weigh the gain and the loss in wagering that God is. Consider these alternatives: If you win, you win all; if you lose, you lose nothing. Do not hesitate, then, to wager that he is." Pascal died at thirty-nine and left behind uncompleted manuscripts concerning the Christian faith. Those notes were later published in 1670 as *Pensées*.

To Be One with God:

O **Lord,** *let me not henceforth desire health or life*
except to spend them for you, with you and in you.
You alone know what is good for me;
do therefore what seems best to you.
Give to me or take from me; conform my will to yours;
and grant that with humble and perfect submission
and in holy confidence I may receive the orders
of your eternal providence, and may equally adore
all that comes to me from you;
through Jesus Christ our Lord. Amen

Søren Kierkegaard (1813-1855) was Denmark's major literary and philosophical figure in the 19th century. Fourteen large volumes make up Kierkegaard's collected published writings, and they fall under the categories of literature, philosophy, theology and devotional thoughts. Although never ordained, many of his writings are quite sermonic. For example, he sounds very much like a pastor when he writes: "Never cease loving a person and never give up hope for him, for even the Prodigal Son who had fallen most low could still be saved. The bitterest enemy and also he who was your friend could again be your friend; love that has grown cold can kindle again." Kierkegaard was the seventh child born into a wealthy family and lived in Copenhagen nearly all of his life. Although he lived a comfortable life, Kierkegaard struggled with depression and guilt. This may have been due to the conflicted feelings he felt toward his father as well as the fact that five of his siblings died within a relatively short period of time.

For a Purer Commitment:

O Lord *Jesus Christ,*
save us from the error of wishing to admire you
instead of being willing to follow you
and to resemble you.

For Peace that the World Cannot Give:

O Lord, *calm the waves of this heart;*
calm its tempests.
Calm yourself, O my soul, so that the divine
can act in you.
Calm yourself, O my soul, so that God is able to
repose in you, so that his peace may cover you.
Yes, Father in heaven, often we have found that the world
cannot give us peace, O but make us feel that you are able
to give peace; let us know the truth of your promise:
that the whole world may not be able to take away
your peace.

Alan Paton (1903-1988) came to be respected and widely known as "South Africa's conscience" for his vocal opposition to apartheid. The writer and educator gave up teaching in 1935 to become principal of the Diepkloof Reformatory for young offenders. There he was recognized for promoting enlightened methods of working with young incarcerated men. Upon leaving that post, he published the novel, *Cry, The Beloved Country* in 1948. The book made an immediate impact around the world. An acclaimed biographer, Paton was also president of the Liberal Association of South Africa (1953-68). Paton often reminded his admirers of the importance of service. "No Christian should ever think or say that he is not fit to be God's instrument, for that in fact is what it means to be a Christian. We may be humble about many things, but we may never decline to be used." Like his books and short stories, Paton's prayers also reflect his concerns about racial equality and issues of justice.

To See the Needs of Others:

O Lord, *open my eyes*
that I may see the need of others,
open my ears that I may hear their cries,
open my heart so that they need not be
     without succour.
Let me not be afraid to defend the weak
     because of the anger of the strong,
nor afraid to defend the poor
     because of the anger of the rich.
Show me where love and hope and faith are needed,
     and use me to bring them to these places.
Open my eyes and ears that I may, this coming day,
     be able to do some work of peace for thee.

For the Courage of Our Convictions:

Give us courage, O Lord, to stand up and be counted,
to stand up for others who cannot stand for themselves.
To stand up for ourselves when it is needful to do so.
Let us fear nothing more than we fear thee.
Let us love nothing more than we love thee,
for then we shall fear nothing also.
Let us have no other God before thee,
whether nation or party or state or church.
Let us seek no other peace but the peace which is thine,
and make us its instruments,
opening our eyes and our ears and our hearts,
so that we should know always what work of peace
we should do for thee.

artin Luther King, Jr. (1929-1968), the martyred minister who became America's most visible and important civil rights leader, reluctantly accepted leadership of the Montgomery Improvement Association in December 1955 in its attempt to desegregate public transportation. The success of the Montgomery bus boycott launched King into the national spotlight. King, the son of a prominent black Baptist pastor in Atlanta, studied at Morehouse College, Crozer Theological Seminary, and Boston University where he earned a Ph.D. He was a powerful orator who championed the cause of black civil rights in America. King believed in peaceful protest and nonviolence and was awarded the Nobel Peace Prize in 1964. Among his many statements exhorting nonviolence and pursuing the path of love are these two: "Returning violence for violence multiplies violence, adding deeper darkness to a night already devoid of stars;" and "I have decided to stick with love. Hate is too great a burden to bear." While greeting supporters from a hotel balcony on a visit to Memphis in April 1968, he was shot dead by James Earl Ray, a white supremacist.

For Strength to Love Our Enemies:

O God, *our Heavenly Father,*
Help us never to let anybody or any condition
 pull us so low as to cause us to hate.
Give us strength to love our enemies and do good
 to those who despitefully use us and persecute us.
We thank you for thy Church, founded upon your Word,
 that challenges us to do more than sing and pray,
 but go out and work as though the very answer to our
 prayers depended on us and not on thee.
Then, finally, help us to realize that man was created
 to shine like stars and live on through all eternity.
Keep us, we pray, in perfect peace, help us to walk together,
 pray together, sing together, and live together until
 that day when all God's children, Black, White, Red
 and Yellow will rejoice in one common band of humanity
 in the kingdom of our Lord and of our God, we pray. Amen.

Benediction Prayer:

And now *unto him who is able to keep us from falling*
 and lift us from the dark valley of despair
 to the mountains of hope,
from the midnight of desperation to the daybreak of joy,
 to him be power and authority, for ever and ever. Amen.

Patrick of Ireland (c. 390- c. 461) was born somewhere on the west coast of England or Scotland—accounts of his origin differ widely. It is generally believed that he was the son of a deacon named Calpurnius. At sixteen he was captured in a raid by Irish pirates and sold to Milchu, a tribal chieftain. For six years Patrick was kept as a slave tending his master's herd. During that time he developed a deep prayer life. "In a single day, I said as many as a hundred prayers," he says in his autobiography. "I used to stay in the woods and on the mountain, and before the dawn I would be aroused to prayer in snow and frost and rain…because then the spirit was fervent within." Patrick escaped and made his way to Gaul where he studied for the priesthood and was sent as a missionary to Ireland by the Pope. He is credited with successfully bringing Christianity to Ireland. Among his early converts was his former master, Milchu. Because much of Patrick's spiritual formation took place while he tended animals in the outdoors, many of his prayers reflect the all-pervasive presence of God.

The Lorica of St. Patrick:

Christ *with me, Christ before me, Christ behind me,*
Christ in me, Christ beneath me, Christ above me,
Christ on my right, Christ on my left,
Christ where I lie, Christ where I sit, Christ where I arise,
Christ in the heart of every one who thinks of me,
Christ in every eye that sees me,
Christ in every ear that hears me.

Salvation is of the Lord,
Salvation is of the Christ,
May your salvation, O Lord, be ever with us.

For the All-Pervasive Presence of God:

May *the strength of God pilot us;*
May the power of God preserve us.
May the wisdom of God instruct us.
May the hand of God protect us.
May the way of God direct us.
May the shield of God defend us.

Pope Paul VI (1897-1963) was born Giovanni Battista Montini near Brescia, Italy, where his prosperous father was editor of a Catholic daily newspaper. He was educated by Jesuits and ordained in 1920. The future Pope went on for further study at the Gregorian University and the University of Rome. Four years later he became part of the Vatican's Diplomatic Corps where his career flourished. From 1937 on he was the Vatican Secretary of State. Montini was appointed archbishop of Milan in 1954 and made a cardinal in 1958. He was elected to succeed the popular Pope John XXIII in 1963 and admirably continued the latter's Vatican II work by convening three more sessions. Under his leadership several remarkable changes were made in the Roman Catholic Church, including abolishing the much-criticized *Index of Prohibited Books,* doing away with the rule against eating meat on Fridays, and replacing Latin Masses with the vernacular. He was the first Pope since 1809 to travel outside Italy and the first to travel by plane.

To Return Good for Evil:

Lord, *God, it is your will that we should love even those who speak or act against us. Help us to observe the commandments of the new law, returning good for evil and learning to forgive as your Son forgave those who persecuted him. Through the same Christ our Lord. Amen*

When Engaged to Be Married:

Father, *in my heart love has come alive for a person you made, and whom you too know and love. It was you who brought me to meet him/her and come to know him/her, as once in paradise you brought Eve and Adam together so that man should not remain alone. I want to thank you for this gift. It fills me with profound joy. It makes me like you, who are love itself, and brings me to understand the value of the life you have given me.*

*Loving Father, I pray for the person who is thinking of me
and waiting for me, and who has placed in me complete trust
for the future; I pray for this person who will walk along the path
of life with me; help us to be worthy of one another and to be
an encouragement and example to one another. Help us
to prepare for marriage, for its grandeur and for its
responsibilities so that the love which fills us body and spirit
may rule our lives evermore.*

Daniel Alexander Payne (1811-1893), whose deep piety and support for education were legendary, was among the first scholars of his denomination, the African Methodist Episcopal Church (AME). Long before he rose to prominence, Payne had a vision of a college where the "peace of God and the light of learning would shine." By age eighteen Payne secured enough education that he could open a school for free blacks in his hometown of Charlestown, South Carolina. His student body numbered three children and three former adult slaves, each of whom paid fifty cents per month tuition. Feeling threatened by educated black people, in 1835 the state of South Carolina made it illegal for any person to operate a school for their education. Disappointed but not discouraged, Payne pursued further education for himself at Lutheran Seminary in Gettysburg, Pennsylvania. In 1844 he joined the AME church in Philadelphia, where he discovered an opportunity to combine his love for religion and education. He was appointed chairman of the church's committee on education. In 1852 he was elected a bishop of the AME church. Because of his commitment to education, Payne was asked to serve as President of Wilberforce University in Ohio, a position he held until 1876. The oldest institution of higher education founded by African-Americans, Wilberforce University is a powerful testimonial to the pioneering spirit of Payne and his AME denomination.

On the Dedication of a Church:

𝔥ear us, *O Merciful Father, and grant that whosoever*
shall be dedicated to you, in this house, by the holy
ordinance of baptism, may also receive the fullness
of your grace, be made useful members of the Church
militant, and finally obtain an abundant entrance into
the Church triumphant through Jesus Christ, our Lord.

Hear us, O merciful Father, and grant, that whosoever shall,
in this house, partake of the symbols of the Saviour's
broken body and shed blood, may also realize by faith,
that he is indeed the Lamb of God, that takes away the
sin of the world, and thus being regenerated and sanctified,
stand spotless and life-crowned, at your right hand,
world without end.

Hear us, O you who are the spouse of the Church, and grant
that whosoever shall, in this house, be joined together in
holy matrimony may also live as did Isaac and Rebecca,
in the purest enjoyment of connubial love, mutually assisting
each other in the way to heaven, and training their children
for usefulness in this world, and for glory in that which is to
come, through Jesus Christ our Lord.

Thus, we have dedicated this house unto you, O you that dwell
in heaven, receive it, O receive it, among your earthly
sanctuaries, and grant, that all who may worship you here,
from Sabbath to Sabbath, and from generation to generation,
even our children's children, may feel it to be indeed the house
of God, and the gate of heaven! Amen.

William Penn (1644-1718) was expelled from Oxford University and imprisoned due to his Quaker beliefs. As a result he became a passionate defender of religious liberty. Because of a debt King Charles II owed to his father, Penn was granted land in America and there he founded the state of Pennsylvania, originally a refuge for persecuted Quakers. He is well known for some of his more memorable words, including: "Though our savior's Passion is over, his compassion is not;" and "Patience and diligence, like faith, remove mountains." Penn was deeply concerned by religious and social intolerance, and often asked for God's help to be more sympathetic of diverse viewpoints.

To Be More Understanding:

O God, *help us not to despise or oppose*
what we do not understand.

Reminder of Life After Death:

We give *back to you, O God, those whom you gave to us.*
You did not lose them when you gave them to us
and we do not lose them by their return to you.
Your dear Son has taught us that life is eternal and
love cannot die, so death is only a horizon
and a horizon is only the limit of our sight.
Open our eyes to see more clearly and draw us
closer to you that we may know that we are
nearer to our loved ones, who are with you.
You have told us that you are preparing a place for us;
prepare us also for that happy place, that where you are
we may also be always, O dear Lord of life and death.

enry Scougal (1650-1678) lived a short but influential life. He is often described as Aberdeen's "immortal mystic" because of his small book *The Life of God in the Soul of Man*. It is regarded as the finest devotional classic to come from Scotland. Ironically, Scougal did not intend his writing to be a book. It was initially written in the form of a letter providing spiritual direction to a friend. The letter, which was 20,000 words in length, was read by Gilbert Burnet, bishop of Salisbury, who immediately recognized it as an exceptional spiritual writing. The bishop received Scougal's permission to have it published. Scougal was something of a child prodigy and entered King's College, Aberdeen, at the age of fourteen. His father was the bishop of Aberdeen. By the time Scougal was eighteen, he had earned a Master of Arts degree. Along with intellectual gifts, Scougal was also blessed with a mystic personality, spending much time in prayer, meditation and spiritual reading. In 1674 he was made a professor of divinity at King's College. He spent the rest of his career there until he died on June 13, 1678, a victim of tuberculosis. Scougal willed his books to the King's College library along with a sum of money that helped augment the salary of his successor as professor of divinity at the college.

For Goodness and Love to Overpower Us:

𝕱ill *our souls with such a deep sense and full persuasion of*
those great truths which you have revealed in the gospel
as may influence and regulate our whole conversation.
Oh, that the infinite perfections of your blessed nature and
the astonishing expressions of your goodness and love
may conquer and overpower our hearts that they may be
constantly rising toward you in flames of devout affection,
and enlarging themselves in sincere and cordial love toward
all the world for your sake.

enesius of Rome (c. 275- c. 303) reportedly offered the following extraordinary prayer at the moment of his martyrdom. It is believed to have been recorded by an eyewitness to the event. Genesius was a Roman actor. While playing the role of a Christian about to be baptized (the play was actually an anti-Christian satire performed before the Emperor Diocletian), Genesius was touched by grace and experienced an immediate, dramatic conversion. He publicly confessed his faith in Christ, an act that resulted in his arrest, imprisonment, torture and beheading. In the Roman Catholic Church Genesius of Rome is a patron saint of actors.

Prayer of Adoration:

There is *no King but him whom I have seen; he it is that I worship and adore. Were I to be killed a thousand times for my allegiance to him, I should still go on as I have begun. I should still be his man.*

Christ is on my lips,
Christ is in my heart;
no torment can ever take him from me.

I am very sorry for the mistake I made in sneering at the holy name in holy men and coming so late to worship the true King, thinking I knew better than to be a soldier of his.

aedmon (died c. 680) is author of the oldest surviving Christian prayer in English. The only information available about Caedmon comes from the Venerable Bede (673-755) who writes about Caedmon in his book *A History of the English Church and People.* There we learn that Caedmon tended cattle at Whitby Abbey in Yorkshire. Although he was a tone-deaf laborer at the Abbey, Caedmon experienced the appearance of a mysterious visitor late one night. That entity appeared to Caedmon in the barn, offering him gifts of song and composition. Thus miraculously inspired, Caedmon composed the following prayer, a hymn to the Creator. This prayer was so popular in medieval England that it survived transmission through seventeen manuscripts dating from the eighth to the fifteenth centuries.

Prayer of Praise:

Now *must we praise the Guardian of the Kingdom of Heaven,*
The might of the Creator, and his wisdom,

The work of the Father of Glory; for he, the Eternal Lord,
Appointed each wondrous thing from the beginning.
He, the Holy Creator, first made heaven
*   as a roof for the children of men;*
And afterward he, the Guardian of mankind, the Eternal Lord,
The Almighty Master, fashioned the earth for mortals.

Henry van Dyke (1852-1933) lived his life working a variety of professions. He was a minister, diplomat, professor, journalist, liturgist, poet, essayist and writer of fiction. Educated at Princeton University and graduating from its seminary in 1877, van Dyke became minister of the Brick Presbyterian Church in New York City. In 1913 President Woodrow Wilson appointed him Minister (Ambassador) to Holland and Luxembourg. He left that post in 1916 and the following year became a chaplain in the United States Navy where he held the rank of lieutenant commander. Van Dyke returned to Princeton University in 1919 as a professor of English literature, a position he held until his retirement in 1923. He wrote more than fifty books, the most popular being a Christmas story titled *The Other Wise Man*. Many of van Dyke's statements were repeated and quoted in sermons and speeches by speakers around the country. For example, he is often quoted for saying: "Time is too slow for those who wait, too swift for those who fear, too long for those who grieve, too short for those who rejoice, but for those who love, time is eternity."

To Share in Christ's Triumph:

O **Christ,** *the brightness of God's glory*
*   and express image of his person,*
*   whom death could not conquer, nor the tomb imprison;*
*   as you have shared our mortal frailty in the flesh,*
*   help us to share your immortal triumph in the spirit.*
Let no shadow of the grave affright us and no fear
*   of darkness turn our hearts from you.*

Reveal yourself to us as the first and the last,
the Living One, our immortal Savior and Lord. Amen.

Theodore Parker (1810-1860) ranks with William Ellery Channing as one of the two greatest leaders of the American Unitarian Movement. This graduate of Harvard Divinity School was greatly influenced by the religious philosophies of Kant and Schleiermacher. Parker's preaching and writing aroused the hostility of Boston area clergy who accused him of presenting views in conflict with traditional Unitarian teachings. Parker was a lifelong advocate of temperance, prison reform, education for women and was a leader of the anti-slavery crusades.

For the Triumph of Truth:

We thank you *for the triumph of truth over error,*
  to us so slow, to yourself so sure.
We bless you for every word of truth which has been
  spoken the wide world through, for all of right which human
  consciences have perceived and made into institutions.
We thank you for that love which will not stay its hold
  till it joins all nations and kindreds and tongues and people
  into one great family of love.

Jeremy Taylor (1613-1667) is sometimes referred to as the "Shakespeare of English Divines" due to the beauty of his writing style. Born in Cambridge, Taylor entered the university there in 1626. One of his fellow students was John Milton, with whom he would drastically differ on matters of politics and theology. Ordained in 1633, Taylor was made a chaplain to King Charles I. During the English Civil War in 1642, Taylor served with royalist forces and was briefly a prisoner of war. Upon his release, he found a new patron, the Earl of Carbery, who made him his chaplain and invited him to live within the safety of his castle. There Taylor began writing books that would bring him fame. He wrote *Holy Living* in 1650 in which he said that holy living requires people to limit their attractions to this world and thereby gain a heavenly destiny. A year later he published *Holy Dying*, reinforcing his view that heaven is reserved only for those who lived in a sober and godly way during their time on earth. In 1660 he was consecrated bishop of Down and Connor (Ireland). His final days were filled with conflicts. As an Anglican bishop, he took issue with Presbyterian clergy as well as with Roman Catholic priests. Somewhat ahead of his time, Taylor urged men to work at developing healthy relationships with their wives and children. "A husband's power over his wife is paternal and friendly, not magisterial and despotic," he said. "He that loves not his wife and children feeds a lioness at home and broods a nest of sorrows."

Prayer During Holy Week:

Grant, *O Lord, that in your wounds I may find my safety,*
in your stripes my cure,
in your pain my peace,
in your Cross my victory,
in your Resurrection my triumph,
and a crown of righteousness
in the glories of your eternal kingdom.

To Be Peaceable and Pious:

Let no *riches make me ever forget myself,*
no poverty make me to forget you;
let no hope or fear, no pleasure or pain,
no accident without, no weakness within,
hinder or discompose my duty,
or turn me from the ways of your commandments.
O let your Spirit dwell with me for ever,
and make my soul just and charitable, full of honesty,

full of religion, resolute and constant in holy purposes,
but inflexible to evil.
Make me humble and obedient, peaceable and pious:
let me never envy any man's good, nor deserve to be
despised myself: and if I be, teach me to bear it
with meekness and charity.

renaeus of Sirmium (c. 120- c. 200) was bishop of Sirmium, an ancient provincial capital city in southeastern Europe, some forty miles west of today's city of Belgrade. Very little is known about Irenaeus, however it appears he was not only an early church leader but must have been a man of considerable importance and leadership. His visibility brought him to the attention of authorities during the persecution under Emperor Diocletian. As a Christian and city leader, Irenaeus was brought before the provincial governor. He was ordered to prove his loyalty to the state by sacrificing an offering to the gods. Upon his refusal he was imprisoned and tortured. Irenaeus was married, as accounts report that his wife and children pleaded with him to save his life by consenting to the governor's demand. Evidently he refused their pleas and was executed.

A Martyr's Prayer of Gratitude:

Thanks *be to you, Lord Jesus Christ:*
in all my trials and sufferings you have given me
the strength to stand firm; in your mercy you have
granted me a share of eternal glory.

For Safety from Evil:

O **Lamb** *of God, who takes away the sin of the world,*
look upon us and have mercy upon us; you are yourself
both Victim and Priest, both Reward and Redeemer,
keep safe from all evil those whom you have redeemed,
O Savior of the world.

Theresa of Lisieux (1873-1897) experienced a profound mystical experience as a teenager, an event that she referred to as her "conversion." Following that experience she shared with her father a desire to enter the Carmelite convent in their town of Lisieux. Her father consented, but both the Carmelite authorities and the local bishop refused due to her young age. A few months later, while in Rome on a pilgrimage with her father, she was at a public audience with Pope Leo XIII. When her turn came to kneel for a papal blessing, Theresa boldly broke the rule of silence mandated for such occasions and asked the Pope: "In honor of your jubilee, allow me to enter Carmel at fifteen." While the Pope was impressed with her piety and determination, he upheld the decision of local church authorities. A year later, however, the bishop gave permission and on April 9, 1888, Theresa entered the convent. Her two devotional books, *The Little Way* and *The Story of A Soul,* were widely and well received. She contracted tuberculosis and died in 1897. Her dying words were: "My God, I love you." She was canonized in 1925 and, together with Joan of Arc, is a patron saint of France.

Longing for God:

Lord Jesus, *I am not an eagle.*
All I have are the eyes and the heart of one.
In spite of my littleness, I dare to gaze at the sun of love,
and long to fly toward it.

When Feeling Sadness:

My God, *I know that I deserve this feeling of sadness;*
however, let me offer it to you, just the same,
as a trial that you have sent me through love.
I am sorry for what I have done,
but I am happy to have all this suffering to offer you.

Woodrow Wilson (1856-1924) once observed: "The object of love is to serve, not to win." The twenty-eighth President of the United States (1913-1921) was born into a staunchly Presbyterian family. His father Joseph Ruggles Wilson was a Presbyterian minister in Georgia. Woodrow Wilson graduated from Princeton University, studied law at the University of Virginia, and earned a Ph.D. in government and history at Johns Hopkins University in 1886. He began teaching at Princeton University in 1890, serving in that capacity until 1902 when he was chosen president of the university. While at Princeton he gained a national reputation through his speeches and writings on popular political issues of the day. He won his bid for governor of New Jersey and from there sought the U.S. Presidency, serving two terms as President. Wilson was an idealist who worked hard to keep America out of World War I. He tried, unsuccessfully, to negotiate peace between Germany and warring nations. Meanwhile, his anti-war stance was becoming increasingly unpopular in the country. Unable to resist the pressure of events and public opinion, on April 12, 1917, Wilson reluctantly asked Congress for a declaration of war. This was passed by an overwhelming majority. As the war ended, Wilson became a leading proponent for the formation of the League of Nations, a body composed of nations from around the world who would work to avert future wars.

For Wisdom in International Affairs:

Almighty God, *supreme Governor of all,*
incline your ear, we beg you, to the prayer of nations,
and so overrule the imperfect counsel of human
beings, and set straight things they cannot govern,
that we may walk in paths of obedience to places of vision,
and to thoughts that purge and make us wise;
through Jesus Christ our Lord.

John Cosin (1594-1672) compiled a work titled *Collection of Private Devotions* that brought him into disfavor with England's rising Presbyterians. Ordained in 1625, he quickly became known for his fierce Anglican loyalties and antagonism toward "non-conformist" churches. When Presbyterian politicians gained complete political power in England after 1641, Cosin moved to Paris where he was chaplain to the exiled royal family. Even there he became known for his debates and quarrels with Roman Catholics. After the Puritan rule of England (1649-1660) and with the restoration of Charles II, Cosin again assumed authority in the English (Anglican) church. In 1660 he was made bishop of Durham. Although he made some attempts to reconcile Presbyterian views with those of his own Church of England, he nevertheless forced both Presbyterians and Roman Catholics to adhere strictly to Anglican forms of worship. A gifted writer, many of his liturgical phrases were incorporated into the *Book of Common Prayer's* revisions. Along with some devotional and liturgical writings, Cosin's other works were mainly polemical pieces largely refuting Catholic positions. In spite of his abrasiveness with other religious groups, Cosin's prayers reveal a kinder and softer side.

For Children:

Almighty God *and heavenly Father,*
we thank you for the children whom you have given to us;
give us also grace to train them in your faith, fear and love,
that as they advance in years they may grow in grace
and be found hereafter in the number of your elect children;
through Jesus Christ our Lord

At the Time of Death:

Into *your hands, O merciful Savior, we commend the soul*
of your servant now departed from the body.

Acknowledge, we humbly beg you,
a sheep of your own fold,
a lamb of your own flock,
a sinner of your own redeeming.
Receive him/her into the arms of your mercy,
into the blessed rest of everlasting peace and
into the glorious company of saints in light.

ohn of Damascus (c. 650-754) served in the caliph's court as minister of Christian affairs in Muslim-occupied Syria, a post held first by his father. He retired in 725, when a movement to exclude Christians from government offices gained momentum, and entered the monastery of St. Sabas near Jerusalem. Later he was ordained as a priest and wrote various books including *Source of Knowledge*, a theological work that catalogues various heresies. Many of his hymns and prayers are still used in Eastern and Western churches. Concerning God's goodness, John wrote: "God who knows everything, and provides for each one of us what will be profitable for us, has revealed what it was to our profit to know; but what we could not bear to know he has kept secret."

Before Receiving Holy Communion:

My heart *is wounded, O Master;*
my zeal for you has melted me away;
my love for you has changed me;
my utter devotion has bound me to you.
let me be filled with your flesh;
let me be satiated with your living and deifying blood;
let me enjoy whatever is good;
let me delight in your divinity;
let me become worthy to meet you
as you come in glory,
and let me be caught up by the clouds, in the air,
together with all your chosen ones,

that I may praise, worship, and glorify you
in thanksgiving and doxology,
together with your Father,
who is without beginning,
and your all holy, good and life-creating Spirit,
now and ever and unto the ages of ages.

Affirming God's Acceptance:

𝕳𝕠𝕨 𝕸𝕬𝕹𝖄 *times, after I had sinned,*
you comforted me, as a good father,
and you kissed me warmly as a son or a daughter,
and you stretched out your arms to me and cried out:
rise up, fear not, stand up, come!

Bonaventure (1221-1274) possessed one of the most outstanding minds of the Middle Ages. Born in Italy, he joined the Franciscan order in 1238 and then went to Paris where he studied under Alexander of Hales. Upon completing his education he was invited to be a professor of theology. After teaching from 1248-1255, Bonaventure became general, or director, of the Franciscan order. Although theologically trained, Bonaventure's spiritual life was characterized more by joy and less by doctrinal matters. For Bonaventure, reason alone could not lead a person to God. Human knowledge needed to be complemented by a spiritual turning toward God. As an example, he once advised: "If you wish to know how such things come about, consult grace, not doctrine; desire, not understanding; prayerful groaning, not studious reading; the Spouse, not the teacher; God, not man; darkness, not clarity." He was regarded as a deeply pious individual, as a theologian of considerable depth, and as a wise administrator. Bonaventure diligently worked to bring together diverse elements and factions that had arisen in the Franciscan order. His important writings include *The Journey of a Soul unto God* and *The Perfection of Life.*

Offering Space for God in One's Life:

O my *God Jesus, I am in every way unworthy of you.*
Yet, like Joseph of Arimathea, I want to offer
a space for you.

He offered his own tomb. I offer my heart.
Enter the darkness of my heart, as your body entered the
darkness of Joseph's tomb. And make me worthy to
receive you, driving out all sin that I may be filled with
your spiritual light.

For a Deeper Understanding of Jesus:

O Lord, *holy Father, show us what kind of man it is who*
is hanging for our sakes on the cross,
whose suffering causes the rocks themselves
    to crack and crumble with compassion,
whose death brings the dead back to life.

Let my heart crack and crumble at the sight of him.
Let my soul break apart with compassion for his sufferings.
Let it be shattered with grief at my sins for which he dies.
And finally let it be softened with devoted love for him.

ertrude More (1606-1633) followed in the spiritual
tradition of her great-great grandfather, Sir
Thomas More. Sensing a call to the religious life,
Gertrude More became a British Benedictine nun
in 1623. At the time her order was in its infancy,
and More was first among nine women admitted to the new
order. After some struggle adjusting to monastic life, More's in-
terior life began to grow and others sought her out for spiritual
counsel. She came down with smallpox in 1633 and died. Some
papers were found after her death that were organized and pub-

lished in two separate works: *The Holy Practices of a Divine Lover* and *Spiritual Exercises.*

Gratitude for Prayer:

(D)ake us *grateful, O God,*
for your grace of prayer;
whereby we have our conversation in heaven;
whereby all impediments are removed,
so that nothing can separate us from your goodness,
for time and eternity.

A lcuin of York (c. 735-804) had a mind that encompassed many disciplines. By the time of his death in France, his literary works included manuals of grammar, rhetoric, orthography, mathematics, biographies of Saints Willibord and Martin of Tours, books of biblical exegesis, and a major work on the Trinity. Born in York, England, Alcuin was educated at the cathedral school where his principal teacher was Albert, a later archbishop of York. Alcuin succeeded him in 766 as head of the school. Impressed by his skills as an educator, Charlemagne, king of the Franks, invited him to leave England and serve in his court in France as his advisor. One responsibility assigned to him by Charlemagne was the instruction of the clergy, particularly monks, in the Latin language, culture and theology, all of which had been significantly eroded over the previous century. After a brief return to England, Alcuin was once again called back to France by Charlemagne in order to overcome various heretical controversies which were raging. He advised the clergy: "You should not listen to those who keep saying that the voice of the people is the voice of God, since a riotous crowd is always next door to madness." Even though he spent the rest of his life in France, in England a society known as the Alcuin Club was formed in his honor. Members met in order to study and promote what they saw as proper worship in the churches.

For Moral and Spiritual Strength:

𝕰𝖙𝖊𝖗𝖓𝖆𝖑 𝕷𝖎𝖌𝖍𝖙, *shine into our hearts;*
Eternal Goodness, deliver us from evil;
Eternal Power, be our support;
Eternal Wisdom, scatter the darkness of our ignorance;
Eternal Pity, have mercy upon us;
    that with all our heart and mind and soul and strength
    we may seek your face and be bought
    by your infinite mercy to your holy presence;
    through Jesus Christ our Lord.

Amnesty International (1961-) is an international organization headquartered in London, England. Its mission is to inform public opinion about violations of human rights with a specific focus upon limits to freedom of speech and religion, as well as the torture and other mistreatment of political prisoners. The organization was established in London on May 28, 1961, through the efforts of Peter Benenson who became aware of the plight of political prisoners when he served as their lawyer. Benenson represented political prisoners in Hungary, South Africa and Spain. From 1961 through 1975 the chairperson of Amnesty International was Sean MacBride, who received the 1974 Nobel Peace Prize.

For Political Prisoners and Their Oppressors:

𝕷𝖔𝖗𝖉 𝕵𝖊𝖘𝖚𝖘, *you experienced in person torture and death*
as a prisoner of conscience. You were beaten and flogged
and sentenced to an agonizing death though you had done
no wrong.

Be now with prisoners of conscience throughout the world.
Be with them in their fear and loneliness, in the agony
of physical and mental torture, and in the face of

execution and death. Stretch out your hands in power
to break their chains.

Be merciful to the oppressor and torturer and place a new heart
within them. Forgive all injustice in our lives and transform us
to be instruments of your peace, for by your wounds we are
*   healed.*

Edward White Benson (1829-1896) was the first Anglican bishop to employ a full-time diocesan evangelist. This took place while Benson was bishop of Truro in Cornwall, England. Born in Birmingham, Benson studied theology at Trinity College, Cambridge. As bishop he proved to be an effective and efficient administrator, inaugurating many new programs and ministries. A perceptive observer of human behavior, Benson wrote: "How desperately difficult it is to be honest with oneself. It is much easier to be honest with other people." Popular with both clergy and laity, Benson became Archbishop of Canterbury in 1882. While in that post, he was forced to preside over a sensational church trial concerning Edward King, bishop of Lincoln, who was charged with "illegal ritualism." After all evidence was presented, Benson decided in favor of the bishop. Throughout his life and ministry, Benson's role model was Cyprian, an early bishop of Carthage. After Benson's death, his own study of Cyprian was published.

Prayer of Confession:

We confess *to you, O heavenly Father,*
*   as your children and your people,*
*   our hardness, and indifference, and impenitence;*
*   our grievous failures in your faith*
*   and in pure and holy living;*
*   our trust in riches and our misuse of them,*
*   our confidence in self, through which we daily multiply*
*   our own temptations.*

We confess our timorousness as your Church and witness before
the world, and the sin and bitterness that all know in
their own hearts.

Give us all contrition and meekness of heart, O Father,
grace to amend our sinful life, and the holy comfort
of your Spirit to overcome and heal all our evils;
through Jesus Christ our Lord.

For a Humble Sense of Self:

Teach me, *good Lord:*

Not to murmur at multitude of business or shortness of time.
Not to magnify undertaken duties by seeming to suffer
under them, but to treat all as liberties and gladnesses.
Not to call attention to crowded work, or petty fatigues.
Not to gather encouragement from appreciation by others,
lest this should interfere with purity of motive.
Not to seek praise, respect, gratitude, or regard from
superiors or equals on account of age or past service.
Not to let myself be placed in favorable contrast with another.

John Chrysostom (c. 347-407) is regarded as one of the greatest preachers in Christianity and certainly the greatest preacher of the early church. Born in Syrian Antioch, he died in exile in the small town of Comanta (today's Pontus in Turkey). His family of birth, while not wealthy, was able to finance an exceptional education for John. He studied philosophy, logic and rhetoric with the aspiration of becoming a lawyer. Through the influence of a classmate, John became interested in spiritual matters and wished to live a monastic life. Those spiritual ambitions, however, had to be delayed as he undertook the responsibility of caring for his widowed mother. Even while residing at home he lived a modified ascetic rule. Around 373 he left to live in the mountains where he spent nearly ten years living a hermetic existence. When his health began to trouble him, John returned to

Antioch, studied under the local bishop (Melitius), was ordained a deacon in 381 and a priest five years later. Very early in his ministry, John exhibited unusually fine gifts for preaching. His most famous series of sermons, *On the Statues,* was delivered in 387 after a major tax revolt took place. Parts of the city were destroyed and several statues of the emperor and his family were desecrated. The people of the city feared imperial retribution. It was John's able and comforting preaching that helped restore order and guide the city calmly through the crisis. When the bishop of Constantinople died in 397, John was appointed to replace him. Unwilling to accept, he avoided going to Constantinople until his capture by the emperor's troops. He was consecrated bishop in 398 and worked hard at clergy and church reform, often taking unpopular positions. At one point he offended the empress Eudoxia and was removed from office and exiled. He returned to Constantinople only to be exiled a second time. He died while in exile. To people who found themselves occasionally experiencing conflicts and troubled by them, John often reminded: "You are a poor soldier of Christ if you think you can overcome without fighting, and suppose you can have the crown without the conflict."

To Enlighten Our Darkened Reasoning:

I **am** *not worthy, Master and Lord, that you should come beneath the roof of my soul: yet, since you in your love toward all wish to dwell in me, in boldness I come. You command, open the gates— which you alone have forged; and you will come in with love toward all as is your nature; you will come in and enlighten my darkened reason. I believe that you will do this: for you did not send away the harlot that came to you with tears; nor cast out the repentant publican; nor reject the thief who acknowledged your kingdom; nor forsake the repentant persecutor, a yet greater act; but all of those who came to You in repentance, were counted in the band of your friends, who alone abide blessed forever, now and unto the endless ages.*

homas Coke (1747-1814) has been described as the "little Doctor" because he stood five feet, one inch. Born to a financially prosperous family in Brecon, Wales, Coke graduated from Oxford in 1768 where he received a B.A., M.A., and Doctorate of Civil Law. He began his ministry as an Anglican curate, but after a fortuitous meeting with one of John Wesley's Methodist evangelists, Coke's preaching became more passionate. He was eventually dismissed from his parish in 1776 for being too "fervent" in his preaching. Coke promptly joined the Methodists and was soon appointed Wesley's secretary and assistant. In 1784 Wesley made a historic decision to appoint Coke as superintendent, overseeing the rapid spread of Methodism in America. At a Christmas conference in Baltimore, Coke became the first American Methodist bishop. Coke made nine voyages from England to the United States. While in America he constantly spoke out against slavery. After his last trans-Atlantic journey, Coke felt called to mission work in Ceylon. In order to prepare for this new endeavor, he donated the last of his personal fortune, some 6,000 pounds, for the effort. As he sailed toward Ceylon, he wrote in his diary: "I am now dead to Europe, and alive for India. God himself has said to me, 'Go to Ceylon!' I am as much convinced of the will of God in this respect as that I breathe.... I had rather be set naked on the coast of Ceylon, without clothes, and without a friend, than not to go there." Coke died on May 3, 1814 en route to Ceylon and his body was buried at sea.

For a Persecuted Church:

O God, *upon my bended knees, I pray you, to remove the iron hand of persecution, which now rests upon thy little flock. Can it be consistent with your holy attributes that these should perish through the malignity and wickedness of your enemies? That is far from you, to do after this manner, to slay the righteous with the wicked. Shall not the Judge of all earth do right?*

Origen of Alexandria (c. 185- c. 254) is often referred to as the "first systematic theologian" of Christianity. Born into a Christian family, he was the oldest of seven children. His father, proud of his son's academic abilities, home schooled him in both secular and religious literature. After his father was martyred, Origen supported his family through his teaching. His classes were so popular and well attended that he divided them into two groupings. Beginners were taught by his assistants, while he worked primarily with advanced students. Origen traveled widely during his life, visiting Rome, Palestine and parts of Arabia. His range of learning was vast, encompassing Biblical exegesis, Hebrew and secular philosophies. Well-known for his efforts to connect neo-Platonic thought with Christian theology, he once wrote: "When Plato says that it is difficult to see the maker and Father of the universe, we Christians agree with him. And yet he can be seen: for it is written, 'Blessed are the pure in heart, for they shall see God.' Moreover, he who is the image of the invisible God has said, 'He who has seen me has seen the Father.'" He produced Christianity's first systematic theology, titled *De Principiis*. Because of his enormous literary output, he was both admired and reviled by other scholars and church leaders. Toward the end of his life, sometime after 250, he was seized by civil authorities who imprisoned and tortured him in an effort to force him to renounce his faith. He refused and was released but died a short time later, possibly due to the physical abuse he endured.

To Put Biblical Knowledge into Daily Practice:

Lord God, *let us keep your Scriptures in mind and meditate on them day and night, persevering in prayer, always on watch.*

We beg you, Lord, to give us real knowledge of what we read and to show us not only how to understand it, but how to put it into practice, so that we may deserve to obtain spiritual grace, enlightened by the law of the Holy Spirit, through Jesus Christ our Lord,

whose power and glory will endure throughout all ages.
Amen.

Lancelot Andrewes (1555-1626) was one of the translators of the King James Version of the Bible. A graduate of Cambridge University, he was ordained in 1580. Andrewes was a person of immense piety, great intellect, and a staunch defender of the Church of England against Rome. He was appointed chaplain to Queen Elizabeth, dean of Westminster (1603), and bishop of Chichester (1605). He was a preacher, teacher, poet and writer of theological books. Among many Anglicans he is regarded as a saint whose feast day is celebrated on either September 25 or 26. His life of meditation and prayer was clearly demonstrated when, after his death, his *Private Devotions* was published. Archbishop Laud referred to Andrewes as "the great light of the Christian world."

For Church Unity:

O Lord, *we pray for the universal church,*
  for all sections of your church throughout the world,
  for their truth, unity and stability,
  that love may abound and truth flourish in them all.
We pray for our own church, that what is lacking
  in it may be supplied and what is unsound corrected;
  and unto all men everywhere give your
  grace and your blessing; for the sake of
  Jesus Christ, our only Lord and Savior.

For Openness to God:

Open *my eyes that I may see,*
Incline my heart that I may desire,
Order my steps that I may follow
The way of your commandments.

J ane Austen (1775-1817) is one of England's greatest novelists. She was born into a home where learning and education was greatly valued. Fortunately for Austen, her parents could afford to educate all seven of their children. She began writing as a child and before age sixteen is reported to have composed sophisticated stories. Her novels, which include *Pride and Prejudice, Sense and Sensibility,* and *Northanger Abbey,* were not especially popular in her lifetime, though she received generous reviews from Sir Walter Scott and Thomas Babington Macaulay. Today, however, her works are highly regarded and continue to be included in many school curricula. Austen's health was often an issue and she frequently experienced weakness, fatigue, and weight loss. She died at forty-two from what is believed to have been Addison's Disease. She was buried in Winchester Cathedral. Although not well known for her piety, Austen nevertheless did pray and took the time to pen several prayers:

To Think and Act Humbly

Incline *us O God!*
to think humbly of ourselves,
to be saved only in the examination of our own conduct,
to consider our fellow-creatures with kindness,
and to judge all they say and do with charity
which we would desire from them ourselves.

To Be Heard When We Pray:

Grant us *grace, almighty Father,*
to pray so as to deserve to be heard.

Thomas Bradwardine (1290-1349) studied theology, philosophy, mathematics and astronomy at Merton College in Oxford University. Upon graduation, he became a lecturer at Oxford and was then appointed chancellor of St. Paul's Church in London. Rising rapidly in church rank, he was chaplain to Edward III and in 1349 was chosen to be Archbishop of Canterbury. He died within weeks of his consecration, however. Bradwardine was a major proponent of the theology of St. Augustine and is viewed as a pivotal leader of an academic movement that restored Augustinian theology in his day.

To Love God at All Times:

Grant, *most gracious God, that we may love you*
always and everywhere,
above all things and for your sake,
in this present life, and at length find you
and forever hold you fast in the life to come.

Ernest T. Campbell (1931-) was senior minister of the Riverside Church in New York City. He was educated at Bob Jones University as well as Princeton Theological Seminary. A lifelong pastor, he served churches in York, Pennsylvania, and Ann Arbor, Michigan, before becoming the senior minister at Riverside. Dr. Campbell was a frequent guest preacher on NBC's "National Radio Pulpit" and "The Protestant Hour." Although now retired, he continues to preach all over the world. His published prayers were initially prepared for worship at the Riverside Church. They reveal a deep pastoral and personal concern for those in his "parish," the residents and workers of New York City.

For the City:

We pray, *Lord, for our city, your gift to us:*
rich in buildings, but, oh, so poor in soul;

high in crime and low in morale;
a playground for some and a nightmare for many;
gateway to the nation, but road's end for those too drugged,
too poor, too tired to get up and try again.
We pray for our mayor, our chief of police, our civil magistrates,
our planners and advisors, that in these crisis years they may
govern and direct us with wisdom, boldness and imagination.
Let the stark prospect of a shared demise unite all who would
build against those who would destroy.

And, if it please You, God, let Your saving grace so reach
and ransom every heart,
that our homes may be joyful,
our streets safe,
our laws just,
our pleasures pure,
and our will to make things right indomitable.
Through Jesus Christ our Lord.

For Society's Helpers:

We pray today for those in our society who have direct
personal contact with men and women, boys and girls,
weighted down with problems:
the social worker, trying to build solvency and hope into families
that cannot make it on their own;
the policeman, called at the eleventh hour to a scene of strife
and danger to settle a dispute he did not cause;
the judge in his chambers quietly interpreting to children
the meaning of a divorce just granted;
the librarian attempting to awaken an interest in serious reading
in young minds addicted to TV;
the guidance counselor pleading with a would-be dropout to
give it another try;
the doctor nurturing the will to live for patients
in the sunset years;

the church-school teacher using every skill of mind and
imagination to bring her students to faith in Jesus Christ.
Encourage them in their work, O Lord, lest in a world of complex
systems and distorted values they should feel their work in vain.
Through Jesus Christ our Lord.

eorge Fox (1624-1691) was founder of the Society of Friends, commonly referred to as Quakers. Born into the family of a weaver in Leicestershire, England, Fox had no formal education but was apprenticed to a shoemaker. A sensitive and spiritually oriented teenager, he was concerned and critical of the major religious movements of his day, especially the Church of England which he believed had lost much of its passion and power because it had become the state church. Fox felt there had to be something more spiritually authentic. He left home at age nineteen in search of spiritual enlightenment. The next three years were challenging for Fox but he discovered "the One" who spoke to his spirit and began to talk about the "Inner Light of the Living Christ" available to all people. In 1647 he began a preaching ministry. Fox traveled widely and quickly gained followers. His main teaching was that spiritual truth was revealed directly by God to the soul of an individual. Fox wanted to revitalize Christianity and reform the Church of England. He declared, "Christ has been too long locked up in the Mass or in the Book; let him be your prophet, priest and king. Obey him." In his *Journal*, Fox wrote: "The Lord opened unto me that being bred at Oxford or Cambridge was not enough to fit and qualify men to be ministers of Christ." Such sentiments aroused hostility from established religious leaders, and in response he founded the Society of Friends in 1652. Because his followers sometimes became physically emotional during services, his society was nicknamed "Quakers." Fox was charged with heresy and jailed in 1649. Until the passing of the Toleration Act in 1689, Quakers were frequently imprisoned for their religious convictions. By the time of his death, the Society of Friends had grown in numbers and influence, counting among their group William Penn, founder of what is now Pennsylvania.

To Forgive Persecutors:

ℰternal *source of love and forgiveness,*
direct us to have the spiritual insight
to know that men who try to harm us
are in need of our forgiveness and mercy.
May we realize that the way to destroy a personal enemy
is by overcoming evil with good,
by praying for those who persecute us.
May we never forget our Master on the cross,
as He was was able to say to His malefactors,
'Father, forgive them, for they know not what they do.'
In the name of this matchless One. Amen.

To Be Living Epistles:

Infinite *source of wisdom,*
we realize that we are 'living epistles,'
who are to carry your Word among men.
Some of us are teachers, or artists, or business leaders,
or writers, or preachers of the Gospel, or mechanics,
or tillers of the soil, or housewives, or students.
Yet we are all 'preachers' of your Word; for we know as
there are many manifestations of your Spirit. Help us to
realize that in our several vocations and professions we
do not build the Kingdom of God: rather as your servants
we receive your Kingdom. May we see living as a great
adventure in which, as we cooperate with you, we 'preach'
you in everything we do in the office, the home, the market
place, the classroom, the church, the great outdoors;
through Jesus Christ our Lord. Amen.

icholas Herman (1611-1691) is better known as Brother Lawrence. Born in Lorraine, France, he spent eighteen years in the army, much of it engaged in the Thirty Years War. There he saw first-hand the ravages of war in which men, women and children were abused, starved, trampled, hanged, robbed, burned and shot, often with no distinction made between soldiers and civilians. Severely wounded, he left the army and obtained work as a civil servant in Parish. There he became impressed with the spirituality of the Carmelite order. He applied and became a lay brother (Brother Lawrence), serving his community as a cook. He did this for thirty years, never seeking advancement beyond that humble status. He was released from those duties only because of blindness. Herman left behind no large writings, only a few spiritual notes and some letters. Preserved with those are four "conversations" with an M. de Beaufort, grand vicar to Cardinal de Noailles. Within a few years of his death, however, his simple writings were edited into a slim volume and published as *The Practice of the Presence of God.* That work has become a spiritual classic appealing to people of differing Christian and religious viewpoints. The beauty of his little book lies in the theme that all people are always and constantly in the presence of God. This is to be both noted and celebrated. Herman wrote, "The time of business does not differ from the time of prayer; and in the noise and clutter of my kitchen, while several persons are at the same time calling for different things, I possess God in as great tranquility as if I were upon my knees at the Blessed Sacrament."

For the Presence of God While Working:

My God, *you are always close to me. In obedience to you, I must now apply myself to outward things. Yet, as I do so, I pray that you will give me the grace of your presence. And to this end I ask that you will assist my work, receive its fruits as an offering to you, and all the while direct all my affections to you.*

When Dealing with a Difficult Task:

𝕸y 𝕲od, *I cannot do this unless You enable me.*
Give me strength more than equal for the task.
Prevent me from failing and mend what is amiss.
In trusting You, may I give myself completely to the
   task at hand and have no reservations about it.

(This prayer was adapted by the author and is based on Brother Lawrence's second conversation with M. de Beaufort, dated September 28th, 1666.)

Johannes Scotus Erigena (c. 810- c. 877) was a leading theologian and philosopher from the Celtic Christian tradition. Born in Ireland of Scottish parents, his name means "John the Scot from Ireland." Although from Ireland, he spent most of his life teaching in France. Around 847 he was appointed supervisor of the court school of Charles I, King of France. That position gave him the luxury of doing academic work, specifically translating from Greek into Latin the works of early church leader Gregory of Nyssa, the Christian neo-Platonist, as well as preparing commentaries on John's Gospel. In keeping with the Celtic spirituality of Irish Christians, Erigena taught that there was an intertwining of the spiritual and the material, of heaven and earth, of time and eternity. Erigena said this could be discerned in "two shoes," one in creation and the other in the Scriptures. Profoundly influenced by the Gospel of John as well as his Celtic background, Erigena believed the spiritual is not divorced from the natural world but is present in it. By looking closely at nature and at the physical world we can gain a greater understanding of God. As a result of his views, Erigena was accused of heresy, as were many Celtic Christians. The usual charge was that he subscribed to *pantheism,* which literally means "god is all things." In fact, Erigena could more accurately be described as subscribing to *panentheism,* literally "god is in all things." Following his death, various Church councils condemned his teachings.

For God's Help in Coming to God:

O you *who are the everlasting Essence of all things*
beyond space and time and yet within them;
you who transcend yet pervade all things,
manifest yourself unto us, feeling after you,
seeking you in the shades of ignorance.
Stretch forth your hand to help us,
who cannot without you, come to you;
and reveal yourself to us, who seek nothing
except you; through Jesus Christ our Lord.

Ulrich Zwingli (1484-1531) is generally regarded as the founder of the Reformation in Switzerland. He was a contemporary of Martin Luther in Germany, but unlike Luther, Zwingli denied that Christ was physically present in the Lord's Supper. Zwingli was born to a peasant family but due to his considerable intellectual gifts received an education in theology. He was ordained a priest and served as pastor of a church in Glarus (1506-1516). Encouraged by Erasmus to study the Bible more carefully, Zwingli began to speak out against corruption in the Church. Like other reformers in Europe, he asserted that the Bible was the sole rule of faith. Between 1519 and 1528, he led reforms in Zurich, Bern and Basel. A fierce reactionary, he led the movement in Zurich to remove all stained glass, murals, and church organs, and banned the use of music. His more extreme views caused Catholics to band together in opposition, resulting in military conflicts. To force the new views upon Catholic districts, Zwingli even promoted civil war. During one of those conflicts, Zwingli himself was killed in 1531. Extreme and radical in his views, Zwingli was instrumental in extending the Reformation into many parts of German-speaking Switzerland.

During an Illness:

Console me, *Lord God, console me!*
The illness increases,
Pain and fear seize my soul and body.

Come to me then, with your grace,
O my only consolation.
My tongue is dumb, it cannot speak a word.
My senses are all blighted.
Therefore is it time
that you my fight conduct hereafter
since I am not so strong,
that I can bravely make resistance
to the Devil's wiles and treacherous hand.
Still will my spirit constantly abide by you, however he rages.

John Milton (1608-1674) is known as the poet of British Puritans. Along with Shakespeare, some regard Milton as one of the finest poets in the English language. His *Paradise Lost,* which traces the fall of Adam and Eve, is viewed as one of the greatest masterpieces of English religious literature. Educated at Cambridge, he entertained the idea of taking up Holy Orders but did not. He lived during a period of considerable political and religious turmoil. Milton wrote a series of political pamphlets in defense of civil and religious liberty that supported the position of the Cromwell government. Milton suffered considerably for his views. During the British Civil War, when government changed hands, Milton lost his job and for a time was forced into hiding. In addition, he experienced several personal hardships. He was widowed twice. By age forty-seven, he was nearly completely blind. Perhaps because of his own sufferings, he stressed the importance of maintaining a healthy attitude. "The mind is its own place, and can make a heaven of hell, a hell of heaven," he wrote. Milton was able to spend the last decade of his life living quietly and continuing his writing with the help of his third wife, Elizabeth Minsul.

For Illumination:

Holy Spirit *of God,*
who prefers before all temples
the upright heart and pure,
instruct us in all truth;
what is dark, illumine,
what is low, raise and support,
what is shallow, deepen;
that every chapter in our lives may witness
to your power and justify the ways of God.
In the name of Jesus, giver of all grace. Amen.

John of Kronstadt (1829-1908) was a Russian Orthodox priest often described as a "wonder worker" because various healings and miracles were ascribed to his ministry. John was born to poor, devout parents living near Archangel in the far north of Russia. While studying at the Theological Academy in St. Petersburg he intended to do mission work in Siberia, but after much prayer he came to sense that God wanted him to do mission work where he was. Upon ordination in 1855 he remained in the area assigned to a poor parish on the island of Kronstadt in the bay near St. Petersburg. The area was home to a Russian naval base where poverty was rampant, and John's ministry focused on combating disease, hunger, alcoholism and high crime. He remained there for fifty-three years serving as an urban missionary. Through his prayers people experienced healing from various ailments and he became well-known throughout Russia. When Emperor Alexander III was dying, John of Kronstadt was called to be at his side. Although an extremely busy parish priest—often beginning work at four a.m. and continuing until midnight—he managed to do some writing. His most prominent work was *My Life in Christ,* a spiritual diary that was well-received in Russia and translated into English. A copy was presented to Queen Victoria. He is a saint in the Russian Orthodox Church.

God Is Everything:

𝕿𝖍𝖊 𝕷𝖔𝖗𝖉 *is everything to me.*
He is the strength of my heart,
and the light of my mind.
He inclines my heart to everything good;
he strengthens it;
he also gives me good thoughts.
He is my rest and my joy;
he is my faith, hope and love.
He is my food and drink,
my raiment, my dwelling place.

etropolitan Philaret of Moscow (1782-1867) enjoyed a reputation as being one of the leading pulpit orators of his time and country. Born in Kolomna, just outside Moscow, he studied for ordination to the Russian Orthodox priesthood. Upon completion of his course work he was appointed a seminary professor and preacher at a monastery. In 1817 he took monastic vows and was shortly after appointed a bishop, then archbishop and, in 1826, became the Metropolitan of Moscow. As Metropolitan (the Eastern Orthodox rank just below that of Patriarch), he delivered sermons critical of some royal policies and practices, and eventually found himself in imperial disfavor. From 1845 until the accession of Alexander II in 1855, his travel was restricted to the limits of his diocese. A gifted communicator both orally and in writing, he produced several theological, spiritual and pastoral works. In addition, he supervised the publication of the first Russian-language Bible. His *Christian Catechism* was extremely influential and was translated into many of the languages of the Russian empire. He is a saint in the Russian Orthodox church and is remembered on November 19 each year.

At the Start of a Day:

O **Lord,** *grant me to greet the coming day in peace.*
Help me in all things to rely upon your holy will.
In every hour of the day reveal your will to me.
Bless my dealings with all who surround me.
Teach me to treat all that comes to me throughout the day
with peace of soul and with firm conviction that
your will governs all.
In all my deeds and words guide my thoughts and feelings.
In unforeseen events let me not forget that all are sent by you.
Teach me to act firmly and wisely,
without embittering and embarrassing others.
Give me the strength to bear the fatigue of the coming day
with all that it shall bring.
Direct my will, teach me to pray,
pray you yourself in me. Amen.

Stanley Hauerwas (1940-) is a leading American theologian of the late twentieth century. In fact, *Time* magazine named him "America's Best Theologian" in 2001. Hauerwas holds joint appointments at the Duke University Divinity School and the Duke Law School. Born on July 24, 1940 in Dallas, Texas, he is the author of nearly thirty books and hundreds of articles covering scores of topics. Hauerwas avoids highly technical, academic jargon, preferring an easy-to-read style for thinking people. He says the best theology is most often found in sermons, homilies, prayers and popular writing. For him, the task of the theologian is to engage the culture's contemporary issues, utilizing language and expressions accessible to all people. Although a prolific writer and lecturer, Hauerwas expresses a modest view of himself, saying that his rise to prominence is not the result of any special intellectual gifts but simply the drive to "outwork" others. "I still work like a bricklayer," he once said. "I get to work at six in the morning and leave at six at night. It's what I do."

On the Occasion of a Suicide:

We pray *for your mercy for those who have killed themselves.*
We know not their fears, and thus we fear they died alone.
> *They are now yours;*
> *in that is our comfort.*
Comfort all who love them and who will miss their presence.

On the Loss of a Pet:

Passionate Lord, *by becoming one of us, you revealed*
> *your unrelenting desire to have us love you. As we were*
> *created for such love, you have made us to love your creation*
> *and through such love, such desire, learn to love you.*
We believe every love we have you have given us.
> *Tuck's* love of us, and our love of him, is a beacon,*
> *a participation, in your love of all your creation.*
We thank you, we sing your praise, for the wonderful
> *life of this cat. His calm, his dignity, his courage;*
> *his humor, his needs, his patience, his always being there*
> *made us better, made our love for one another better,*
> *made us better love you.*
We will miss him. Help us not fear remembering him,
> *confident that the sadness such memory brings is*
> *bounded by the joy that Tuck existed and, with us,*
> *is part of your glorious creation, a harbinger of your*
> *peaceable kingdom. Amen.*
(* Tuck was a Siamese cat who lived for twenty years.)

ary Elizabeth Sumner (1828-1921) founded the Mothers' Union in England, an association to support the welfare of mothers and children. Sumner was educated by her parents. In 1848, while on holiday in Rome, she met and later married George Sumner. Her husband was an Anglican clergyman who served as chaplain to his uncle, the Archbishop of Canterbury. In 1851, he left that post to become priest of a parish in Alresford, Hampshire. In 1876 Mary Elizabeth Sumner began to hold meetings for mothers. A speech she delivered at a conference in 1885 formally gave rise to the Mothers' Union, beginning in England and spreading worldwide. Under her leadership, the association enjoyed rapid growth. Sumner continued to promote it until her death.

To Be Used Daily by God:

All this day, *O Lord,*

let me touch as many lives as possible for you;
and every life I touch, let your Spirit quicken,
whether through the word I speak,
the prayer I breathe, or the life I live.

oyohiko Kagawa (1888-1960) lived a lonely and desperate life as a youth. Born as an illegitimate child of a Japanese geisha, he suffered greatly in his childhood. At age fifteen, encouraged by missionaries, he converted to Christianity. Family and friends disinherited him for this. Nevertheless, he chose to study for the Christian ministry. While at Kobe Seminary he became seriously concerned for the needs of the underprivileged. After recovering from tuberculosis in 1909, he moved into the slums of Kobe to live and work among the poor. From 1914 to 1916, Kagawa studied at Princeton University and Princeton Theological Seminary. Upon returning to Japan, he devoted himself completely to improving social conditions. He organized the first labor unions in Japan and evangelized in the slums of Kobe. Though ordained a Presbyterian minister, Kagawa was a major ecumenical figure. He opposed the Japanese military and served time in jail during World War II. Gradually, however, the Japanese came to respect him as their nation's conscience. After his death the Emperor granted him the highest designation available for a Japanese citizen. By the time of his death he had authored and translated 169 books on religion, sociology and science.

Prayer of Confession:

𝕲reat 𝕲od, *our Father:*
> *As we call to mind the scene of Christ's suffering*
> *in Gethsemane, our hearts are filled with penitence and shame*
> *that we foolishly waste our time in idleness and that we make*
> *no progress in the Christian life from day to day.*
> *We are ashamed that war and lust flourish and grow more*
> *rampant every day.*
> *Forgive us for our cruel indifference to the cross, and pardon us*
> *that, like the bystanders of old, we merely stand and gaze in*
> *idle curiosity upon the piteous scene.*
> *O teach us, we ask you, the good news of your forgiveness.*
> *Cause humanity, degenerate as it is, to live anew, and hasten*
> *the day when the whole world shall be born again.*

Peter Marshall (1902-1949) was only in his thirties when he began to gain a reputation as one of the most outstanding preachers in North America. Born in Scotland, Marshall emigrated to the United States in 1927, where he studied for the ministry at Columbia Theological Seminary in Decatur, Georgia, from 1928-1931. Six years later, he succeeded the famed Dr. Joseph R. Sizoo as minister of the prestigious New York Avenue Presbyterian Church in Washington, D.C. An enormously gifted and popular preacher, he was appointed chaplain to the U.S. Senate in 1947 and served until his untimely death from a heart attack in 1949. His death stunned the city. The Washington Post reported: "We deplore, as the Capital must, the untimely death of Dr. Peter Marshall…. Till Dr. Marshall came to the Senate two years ago, the Senators had heard a more or less perfunctory sort of grace before they began their deliberations. The Presbyterian minister opened the ears of the bowed Senators to his words of prayer…." After Marshall's death, his wife Catherine wrote a biography titled *A Man Called Peter*. It was a best seller in the early 1950s. Although most of Marshall's published prayers were delivered at the opening daily sessions of the U.S. Senate, many of them contain applications to the lives of ordinary people engaged in their daily activities.

To Fill the Moment of Prayer with Meaning:

We pray, *O God, that You will fill this sacred minute with meaning and make it an oasis for the refreshment of our souls, a window cleaning for our vision, and a recharging of the batteries of our spirits.*
Let us have less talking and more thinking,
less work and more worship,
less pressure and more prayer.
For if we are too busy to pray, we are far busier
than we have any right to be.
Speak to us, O Lord, and make us listen to your broadcasting
station that never goes off the air.

For a Greater Sense of God's Reality:

O God, *our Father, be real to each one of us today, that we may become aware how near you are and how practical your help may be.*
Deliver us from going through the motions as though
waiting for a catastrophe.
Save us from the inertia of futility.
Revive our spirit of adventuresome faith.
Give us nerve again and zest for living,
with courage for the difficulties of peace.
Through Jesus Christ our Lord. Amen.

Albert Schweitzer (1875-1965) did not go to Africa in order to become famous or win the world's admiration. He responded to a divine calling to serve as a medical missionary and left behind what would have been a comfortable life as an academic. Born in the region of Alsace, a contested province straddling the border of France and Germany, Schweitzer was drawn to both intellectual life and a life of service. He earned doctorates in two fields: theology and philosophy. His book *Quest of the Historical Jesus* (1905) quickly established him as a foundational figure in twentieth-century theology. That book fueled future academics to identify the differences in the Jesus of history—as presented in the Gospels—and the Christ of faith as proclaimed by the Church. Along with academic renown, Schweitzer also established himself as a major authority on the music of J. S. Bach. With that background, Schweitzer could have built an extraordinary life and career. After reading a notice about the need for doctors in Africa published by the Paris Missionary Society, however, Schweitzer reflected on his life before telling family, friends and colleagues he would turn to the study of medicine and serve in Africa. Although those in his social circle were convinced he was merely having a mid-life crisis, Schweitzer remained faithful to his call and eventually arrived at Lambarene, a small village on the Ogowe River in today's Gabon. There he supervised the building of a hospital. Schweitzer lived to the age of ninety and died at his hospital on September 4, 1965. For his service to humanity, Schweitzer was awarded the Nobel Prize in 1958. His compassion extended beyond people and included animals. His Christian convictions manifested themselves as reverence toward all life.

For Our Friends the Animals:

Hear *our humble prayer, O God, for our friends the animals,*
especially for animals who are suffering;
for any who are hunted or lost or deserted
or frightened or hungry;
for all that must be put to death.

We ask for them all your mercy and pity and for those who
*   deal with them we ask a heart of compassion, gentle hands*
*   and kindly words.*
Make us ourselves to be true friends to animals and so to
*   share the blessing of the merciful.*

Personal Dedication:

𝕳𝖊𝖗𝖊, *Lord, is my life.*
I place it on the altar today.
Use it as you will.

Works Consulted

Every effort has been made to trace and acknowledge copyright holders of the prayers included in this work. We apologize for any errors or omissions that may remain and invite those concerned to contact the publishers, who will ensure that full acknowledgement is made in the future.

Adams, Russell L. *Great Negroes Past and Present.* Chicago, Illinois: African-American Images Press, 1984.

Appleton, George, ed. *The Oxford Book of Prayer.* Oxford: Oxford University Press, 1985. (Consulted for prayers by Rabi'a, Teilhard de Chardin, Thich Nhat Hanh, Mirabi and Siddhartha Gautama. Used with permission. All rights reserved.)

Appleton, George. *Prayers From A Troubled Heart.* Philadelphia: Fortress Press, 1983.

Buckley, Michael. *The Catholic Prayer Book.* Ann Arbor, Michigan: Servant Books, 1986.

CLC Publications, Fort Washington, PA, and the Donhavur Fellowship for the prayers of Amy Carmichael. Used with permission. All rights reserved.

Cahill, Susan, ed. *Wise Woman.* New York: W. W. Norton Co., 1996.

Campbell, Ernest T. *Where Cross The Crowded Ways: Prayers of a City Pastor.* New York: Association Press, 1973. Used with permission. All rights reserved.

Carden, John. *A Procession of Prayers: Meditations and Prayers from Around the World.* Geneva: World Council of Churches Publications, 1988.

Complete Book of Christian Prayer, The. New York: Continuujm Publishing Company, 1996. (Consulted for the use of prayers by John Baillie, Karl Barth, Eugene Bersier, Dietrich Bonhoeffer, Helder PessoaCamara, John Oxenham, Alan Paton, Mother Teresa of Calcutta, Evelyn Underhill, Albert Schweitzer, Dag Hammarskjold, Toyohiko Kagawa. Used with permission. All rights reserved.)

Craughwell, Thomas J., ed. *Every Eye Beholds You: A World Treasury of Prayer.* New York: Quality Paperback Book Club, 1998.

Davies, Horton, ed. *The Communion of Saints.* Grand Rapids, Michigan: William B. Eerdmans Publishing Company, 1990.

Douglas, J. D., ed. *Who's Who in Christian History.* Wheaton, Illinois: Tyndale House Publishers, 1992.

Draper, Edythe. *Draper's Book of Quotations for the Christian World.* Wheaton, Illinois: Tyndale House Publishers, 1992.

Ellsberg, Robert. *All Saints: Daily Reflections on Saints, Prophets, and Witnesses For Our Time.* New York: Crossroad Publishing Company, 1997.

Hauerwas, Stanley, Durham, NC, for use of his prayers. Used with permission. All rights reserved.

Hobe, Phyllis. *Your Personal Handbook of Prayer.* Philadelphia: Westminster Press, 1982.

Hsu, Albert Y. *Grieving a Suicide.* Downers Grove, IL. Intervarsity Press, 2002.

Jackson, Samuel Macauley, ed. *The New Schaff-Herzog Encyclopedia of Religious Knowledge.* New York: Funk and Wagnalls, 1911.

Job, Rueben and Norman Shawchuck. *A Guide to Prayer for Ministers and Other Servants.* Nashville, Tennessee: Upper Room, 1983.

Kepler, Thomas, ed. *Selections from the Writings of Francois Fenelon.* Pamphlet published by The Upper Room, Nashville, TN, 1962. Used with permission. All rights reserved.

Kepler, Thomas, ed. *Henry Scougal: The Life of God in the Soul of Man.* Pamphlet published by The Upper Room, Nashville, TN, 1962. Used with permission. All rights reserved.

Kepler, Thomas, ed. *Selections From the Journal of George Fox.* Pamphlet published by The Upper Room, Nashville, TN, 1951. Used with permission. All rights reserved.

Kepler, Thomas, ed. *Selections from the Writings of John Bunyan.* Pamphlet published by The Upper Room, Nashville, TN, 1951. Used with permission. All rights reserved.

Lemopoulos, Georges, ed. *Let Us Pray to the Lord: A Collection of Prayers from the Eastern and Oriental Orthodox Traditions.* Geneva: WCC Publications, 1996.

McNally, Thomas, ed. *Lord, Hear Our Prayer.* Notre Dame, Indiana: Ave Maria Press, 1978.

Parachin, Janet W. *Engaged Spirituality: Ten Lives of Contemplation and Action*. St. Louis, Missouri: Chalice Press, 1999.

Potts, Manning, J., ed. *Selections from the Journal of Francis Asbury*. Pamphlet published by the Upper Room, Nashville, TN, 1952. Used with permission. All rights reserved.

Prayers Offered by the Chaplain the Rev. Peter Marshall at the Opening Sessions of the Senate of the United States During the Eightieth and Eighty-First Congresses, 1947-1949. U.S. Government Printing Office, Senate Document No. 86. 1949.

Rice, Howard and Lamar Williamson, eds. *A Book of Reformed Prayers*. Louisville, Kentucky: Westminster John Knox Press, 1998.

Smith, Warren Thomas, ed. *Selections from the Writings of Thomas Coke*. Pamphlet published by The Upper Room, Nashville, TN, 1966. Used with permission. All rights reserved.

Steere, Douglas, ed. *Selections from the Writings of Evelyn Underhill*. Pamphlet published by The Upper Room, Nashville, TN, 1961. Used with permission. All rights reserved.

Steere, Douglas, ed. *The Practice of the Presence of God* by Brother Lawrence. Pamphlet published by The Upper Room, Nashville, TN, 1950. Used with permission. All rights reserved.

Stewart, Dorothy, M. *The Westminster Collection of Christian Prayers*. Louisville, Kentucky: Westminster John Knox Press, 2002. Consulted for prayers by William Barclay. Used with permission. All rights reserved.

Thorne, Leo S., ed. *Prayers from Riverside*. New York: Pilgrim Press, 1983.

University of Massachusetts Press, Amherst, MA, for prayers by W. E. DuBois. Used with permission. All rights reserved.

Walsh, Michael, ed. *Butler's Lives of the Saints*. New York: Harper Collins, 1991.

Ward, Hannah and Jennifer Wild, eds. *The Doubleday Christian Quotation Collection,* New York: Doubleday Publishers, 1997.

Washington, James Melvin. *Conversations with God: Two Centuries of Prayers by African-Americans*. New York: Harper Collins, 1994.

Watkins, Peter and Erica Hughes. *A Book of Prayer*. New York: Franklin Watts Inc., 1982.

Weatherhead, Leslie. *A Private House of Prayer*. Nashville, Tennessee:

Abingdon Press, 1958. © The family of Rev. Dr. Leslie Weatherhead. Used with permission. All rights reserved.

Zundel, Veronica, ed. *Eerdman's Book of Famous Prayers: A Treasury of
Christian Prayers Through the Centuries.* Grand Rapids, Michigan:
William B. Eerdmans Publishing Company, 1983.

Index of Authors

Index of Prayers by Subject

Also from ACTA Publications

A Contemporary Celtic Prayer Book by William John Fitzgerald. A simplified Liturgy of the Hours and a treasury of prayers, blessings and rituals in the Celtic style. (160-page paperback, $9.95)

The Rosary: Mysteries of Joy, Light Sorrow and Glory by Alice Camille. An in-depth and enlightening discussion of the Rosary, its history and significance, including the new Mysteries of Light. (96-page paperback, $6.95)

Prayer: A Practical Guide by Martin Pable. Addresses traditional prayer, praying with the Bible, meditation, contemplation, and the Mass as prayer. (96-page paperback, $9.95)

Praying the New Testament as Psalms by Desmond O'Donnell and Maureen Mohen. Verses from the New Testament are used as the basis for 100 original prayers, each arranged as a psalm-like format. (216-page paperback, $12.95)

A Catholic Prayer Companion CD. A reverent recitation of thirty prayers by two professional narrators, accompanied by beautiful, original background music. Also available in book form. (30-minute compact disc, $12.95; 48-page paperback, $4.95; 48-page large print version, $5.95)

Available from booksellers or call 800-397-2282
www.actapublications.com